'I Am Enough!'

About the Author

Gary Cunningham is a writer, musician, inspirational speaker and author of *Joys of Joy: Finding Myself in an Irish Prison* and *Life After Joy: A Prisoner No More*. He keeps a regular blog which can be found at https://garcunningham.wordpress.com.

'I Am Enough!'

Words to Live By

Gary Cunningham

The Liffey Press

Published by
The Liffey Press Ltd
'Clareville'
307 Clontarf Road
Dublin D03 PO46, Ireland
www.theliffeypress.com

© 2019 Gary Cunningham

A catalogue record of this book is
available from the British Library.

ISBN 978-1-9160998-3-8

Printed in Spain by GraphyCems.

Contents

To all those who think they're not good enough ...
This one is for you

Introduction

I wish I never felt the need to write this book in the first place, which is kind of a strange opening statement for an author to make. But the book you are now holding has come from a place of genuine concern.

I am the author of two other books, *Joys of Joy: Finding Myself in an Irish Prison* and *Life After Joy: A Prisoner No More*, which together provide a snapshot of how badly I handled my life in the past. I am a former inmate of Mountjoy Prison and Loughan House Open Centre, having being sentenced under the *Misuse of Drugs Act 1977* to three and a half years in prison for *the possession of Cannabis with the intent to sell or supply*.

My entire world collapsed when the judge passed down his sentence on March 27, 2012, and yet I had no one to blame but myself. So in prison I embarked on a journey of self-discovery and healing, a journey I am still working on today. I promised myself that I would change every fibre of my being, and that I would do all I could to help those around me. I had lived such a negative, selfish life before prison so I am proud to be forging this new path.

Not long after my release came the publication of my first book, and its success is still something I find completely mind-blowing ... it is currently being adapted for the big screen for feck sake! The success of that book opened up many doors for me, and has allowed me to fulfil a promise made in prison, which is to help others.

It all started with being asked to go back into prisons to give talks about what I had learned. Of course I was nervous, but I felt I had an important, positive message for those who wanted to hear it, and thankfully all the talks I have given in jails to date have been a success. I would encourage the men and women who attended to 'own their shit', to not offer excuses for why they found themselves incarcerated. I would also urge them to believe in themselves, as I am convinced that this makes the process of rehabilitation more achievable. We all make mistakes, but with the right attitude we are also capable of righting our wrongs.

As much as I was honoured to be asked to go into prisons to talk to inmates, I remember thinking, *'I'm a bit late here though, aren't I? I mean, these men and women are already incarcerated. I'd love to go into schools and talk to our youths.'* I believe in the Law of Attraction – ask and you shall receive – so I asked! Skip forward almost a year after my release and I find myself about to take to the stage in Listowel, County Kerry at the 'Young Adult BookFest' in front of 900 fourth- and fifth-year students. No pressure so!

That morning is one I will never forget. It was the very first talk I gave to a large group of students, and I gave it in my unique way. I rant … a *lot*! I use profanity … a *lot*! But the most important thing? I care … a hell of a lot! What happened when I left the stage that morning has happened in every school I have had the honour to speak in since. Almost every young person there who sought me out afterwards thanked me for my talk and then described what was going on in their lives. And sadly, their stories were pretty awful.

I am forty years of age so when I was a teen I didn't have to deal with the toxic side of social media that our youths find themselves dealing with today, all the pressures of 'trying to keep up with the Kardashians' and 'FOMO (Fear of Missing Out)', and the online bullying. It's quite scary. And I refuse to believe that these young adults are just 'moany little shites'. Yes, maybe some are moaning to get attention or just being awkward, but we should ask, 'Why?' And then we should clear our minds and listen. This is what I have chosen to do.

After Listowel word of my talks travelled fast. To date, I have travelled the length and breadth of Ireland volunteering myself to go into schools and YouthReach groups to deliver my message. I stated earlier that I use profanity in these talks, and some adults may find that surprising, even inappropriate. But don't think I stand there effing and blinding for no reason. I just feel that for these students I need to be as real as I can and my sporadic use of profanity – in school, no less! – makes me sound authentic and plays a huge part in the success of my talks.

Sadly, though, the more schools and YouthReach groups I talk to, the more troubled students I have opening up and telling me exactly what they are going through, the more I see a need to truly listen to our young people.

As my talks in schools began gathering momentum, I was struck by the poor self-image many of our youths have of themselves. So I began to think about what my true message should be – my mantra, so to speak. What was the one thing I wanted these students to think and feel once I had finished talking? Well, that was easy. I wanted each and every student to walk away repeating the three words I get them to roar back at me at the end of my talks – 'I Am Enough!' I want them to know how important they are, and that the person they are is *enough*. This has become my trademark. So at the end of my talks, I am usually standing on top of a desk, roaring at the top of my voice as the students repeat after me – 'I Am Enough!'

But there is one shocking story that actually motivated me to write this book.

After one particular talk I gave, I had a queue of students lining up waiting to have a chat with me, which moved me beyond belief. But one brave young lady, whom I shall refer to as 'K', stopped me in my tracks. Our discussion went as follows:

'K' (crying uncontrollably): 'Thank you so much Gary, for telling me I am enough ... I really needed to hear that today.'

Gary: 'But here's the thing missus ... you are actually *more* than enough!'

'K': 'God! I'm so, so sorry I'm crying like this – it's just my best friend committed suicide two weeks ago ...'

I was rooted to the spot. In a daze I turned to her teacher and asked, 'How old is this girl standing in front of me?' Thirteen. Her friend who so tragically took his own life? *Thirteen*.

I haven't been the same since I met 'K' and heard her story. We communicate through Facebook, and I do all I can to help her as she deals with something that I think we can all agree shouldn't be happening. When I was thirteen I couldn't *spell* suicide, and I most certainly didn't know anyone my age who had taken their own life. Yet today? It is happening at an alarming rate.

It was a combination of 'K's' story and the countless messages I received from students telling me their struggles that compelled me to write this book – and I'm writing it for *you*. Because I want you to know, before we even get started, that *You Are Enough!* Yes I will try to highlight the importance of talking about and sharing the sad stories you are about to read, but I feel it must start with how *you* view yourself. So exercise No. 1? Put this book down, head over to a mirror, look at that face staring back at you, and with confidence proudly say out loud, '*I Am Enough!*' Because I promise you truly are.

What follows are all true stories that countless students have shared with me following my talks. The names and details have been changed to ensure their privacy. Not every account will have a happy ending – life can be shit sometimes – but it is how we deal with things that matters. My hope is that these stories will allow you to think differently about certain things, and that you will realise that talking about your feelings and worries is not a sign of weakness but one of strength. At the end of the book is a Personal Reflections section where you can write down any thoughts you might have about what you've read.

I don't for a minute think that I am some feckin' expert or that I have all the answers. In fact, at the back of this book you will find a collection of phone numbers and websites that I urge you to use should you feel the need, especially if you are disturbed by any of the stories in these pages. Each chapter describes some dilemma or trauma that someone had to deal with, and at the end there is a discussion section looking at how the situation was handled. Hopefully, by the end of this book, it will have sparked some useful conversations between you and your friends and family.

And before I sign off, I would just like to say that I recently went back to give another talk in the same school where I first met 'K'. This time I had a whole new bunch of students to talk to, but as I made my way across the schoolyard, I heard my name being called. I turned to see 'K' standing there, and for the first thirty seconds we just had an auld cry. Then I composed myself and told her that her story ripped me apart, and yet it inspired me to write this book.

I said, 'There is nothing positive about your friend taking his own life, 'K', but if we can reach someone else with your story and make them stop and think, wouldn't that be a good thing?'

So 'K'? This one is for you. Thank you for your bravery and strength.

Finally, the picture on the following page (sorry we can't print it in colour) was created by a very special young lady, Hannah, a seventeen-year-old girl currently dealing with her own issues. I got to speak in Hannah's school, and after hearing me talk she painted the picture and posted it to me with a note that read: *'Thank you for giving me this amazing message. I thought it was only fair that someone gives it to you too.'* Yep, I was bawling after reading that.

1.

'Am I Enough?'
– Martin's Story

Monday morning and the rain outside is Biblical. I mean, I've seen rain before, but I've never *heard* rain quite like this, as it almost smashes off the grey concrete outside. '*Typical*,' I think to myself. I was already dreading this particular Monday as it is 'Casual Monday' in school, which means we don't have to wear our uniforms. *Typical!*

'Martin! I won't call you again. Get down here for your breakfast or it'll be feckin' dug outta ya!'

My dad is a cool dad by all accounts, but he doesn't handle pressure too well. And I suppose trying to get myself and my two younger siblings – Amy, nine going on thirty, and Peter, twelve going on twelve and a half – ready for school is a task that would age anyone.

'*Martin*!!' He's getting pissed off now.

'I'm comin' da, I'm comin'. Just gonna fix me hair,' I reply, but truth be known, I'm not even dressed yet. Poxy 'Casual Monday!' At least when I wear my uniform, I kinda look the same as the rest of the lads. But today? Today they're gonna see how poor I am. Today they're gonna have ample ammo to take the piss out of me. Maybe I should pull a sickie? Suddenly, my bedroom door swings open, and there stands my dad, red-faced, his Mayo accent seeming to increase in pitch as he yells at me.

'Ahhh *Jaysis* Martin – sure you're not even *dressed* like! *Will ya come onnn* man!'

He is a great dad to be fair. Things have been pretty crap since mam passed away – almost four years now. It ripped us all apart, but dad took the brunt. And yet, as his kids, we'd never know. He is currently working two jobs, a painter and decorator by day and an office cleaner by night. He wants to do everything he can so we want for nothing, but in truth his two jobs are providing just enough to keep the wolves from the door. So, I try not to add to his worries. But today? Today I'm shittin' man! I don't have the head for all the laughing. I don't have the head for Tommy either. He always has something smart to say, and when he sees my Penny's runners and my Liverpool jersey from two years ago? He's gonna have a bleedin' field day. Tommy and I have never seen eye to eye. Don't get me wrong, he's no bully. I wouldn't let anyone bully me. He's just a spoilt little toe-rag … or is he? Maybe it's me with the problem? Nah! It's not me, it's bleedin' Tommy!

After trying on many different combinations of clothing, I settle for a t-shirt my uncle Jason brought home for me from New York. Yes, it's three years old, but beggars can't be choosers. As I head out of my bedroom, I catch one last sight of myself in the mirror, and I cringe. *Poxy bleedin' 'Casual Monday'*.

I enter the kitchen just as Amy gives Peter a massive clatter across the back of his head for 'annoying her'. Dad looks like he's about to collapse. God ... here I am worried about a pair of runners. Am I really that selfish?

'Ah, so you decided to grace us with your presence Sir Martin,' mocks my dad.

He is a tall, proud man with coal-black hair and, in his own words, a 'cool hipster beard.' Jesus. The embarrassment. I was going to give him a cheeky reply, but instead I just smile. It's not long before we hear the front door opening, followed by the cheerful voice of my Aunty Cody. Aunty Cody is dad's sister, and she has been really there for us since mam passed away. Every morning she arrives, with her own child in tow, to help my dad get Amy and Peter ready for school. Cody's husband, Uncle Dillon, is really cool too. We happen to like some of the same music – music none of my mates seem to 'get' – like The Doors, you know, *'Come On Baby Light My Fire...'*

I say my goodbyes just as Amy begins showing Aunty Cody her new hip-hop dance moves. I step out of my house and into the rain I mentioned earlier ... Jaysus. This rain could be done for assault it's that heavy! At the top of my road, waiting patiently, is my best mate, Andy. Some say we're like twins me and Andy, both tall, skinny rakes with strawberry blonde hair. 'And we're really funny too, don't forget,' is how Andy usually replies to someone comparing us.

'S'up?' asks Andy.

'Feck all man,' I start, 'bar the staaate of me clobber, I mean, just *look at me man!'*

Andy doesn't laugh when he hears this comment. 'And just what is wrong with ya Martin, eh? Ya look grand buddy. Don't be worryin.'

Andy is, hands down, the best mate anyone could ask for. We've been mates since – well, kinda forever really. He's got my back, and I've got his.

'Fifth year really is a load of me hole isn't it man?' laughs Andy.

'Ah stop man,' I start as we battle our way through the rain towards our school, 'and as for 'Casual Monday?' *Ask me arse.*' I start to laugh, but when I look over towards my friend, I see he's not joining me.

'Why do you always worry what people think man?' asks Andy, the concern ringing through his voice. 'And if it's Tommy you're worryin' about? Don't bother man. He's just not worth it.'

Andy never fails to amaze me. He's mad like. I mean, he's not afraid to cry in front of the lads, he *always* says 'I love ya' to his ma when he sees her, and yet, he'd rip your head off if ya stuck it up to him. Me? I never cry – well, never in public anyway.

'Ah, ya know yourself man. It's just the state of me clothes and that, ya know? And you can bet me doing all your homework next week, that Tommy is gonna walk in with feckin' gold plated runners and a mink coat.'

Andy starts to laugh hard, but then composes himself enough and says, 'Who actually cares? I mean, who *really* cares about what clothes you've got on?'

'I do Andy,' I respond, but I can feel the tears coming, so I back down.

'And why do you care? Let me tell ya what me da told me the other day – you're gonna love this one pal. He says to me, *'Opinions are like arseholes son, everyone has one.'* We both fall around laughing. Andy's da is a legend. And maybe he's right too. I just can't shake this feeling of not being good enough.

Double Maths into Biology, and on a Monday morning too. It's like they *want* us to hate this place. Tommy has remained quiet so far, too quiet for my liking. Mr. Malone (Maths) leaves and as he does, Tommy spins around in his chair to face me.

'Nice t-shirt Marty, I hear the year 1999 is looking for it back.' Tommy and his little gang of followers all laugh, but no one else does. Me? I'm rooted to the spot. Why does my life have to be this way? Why am I the one who is poor? Why did today have to be poxy 'Casual Monday'?

Andy jumps in. 'We all can't afford designer gear like you Tommy, but I'll tell ya what. See Martin? As a human, he is a millionaire, whereas you, with the attitude you have towards people? You're a pauper.' A silence descends over the classroom. You would be fooled that a straightener was about to take place. But, thankfully, none of the lads in my year are like that. None of that 'macho bullshit' going on. Like I said before, Tommy is no bully, he's just a gloating fool. So why does he get to me? Why do I let this stuff bother me so much? Why? Why? Why?

Tommy has no answer for Andy, and soon Mr. Shaw (Biology) enters and in the most boring voice you can imagine he says, 'Okay ... lads ... open ... page ... eh ... 243 ... and ... we'll ... ehhhhhh ... get ... started.' Jaysus!

Out in the yard, and Tommy is nowhere to be seen. 'Fair play to ya for sayin' that to Tommy earlier,' I say to Andy as we blend in with the other students.

'Martin?' Andy says, 'I really want you to listen to this okay? Please man.'

I look at my best friend and see he has tears forming at the bottom of his eyelids.

'See you? I've never met anyone like ya Martin. You're kind, funny, sound, a mad fecker! You're giving, understanding, a great brother and son and friend. You're in the top three in our class every year in exams, but most importantly of all, you are always there if someone needs you. So, when I see you down because of your bleedin' t-shirt, when I hear you worry about your runners and I see how upset you get, it makes wanna feckin' shake ya! With your heart, your mind, and your friendship, you are the richest man I know. Think of Tommy. Like, god love him an' all, but he's just a bit of a sap. No one goes to him for advice like the way they come to you. No one looks up to him like they do to you. You lost your mam, and yet you have been there for so many of us ever since. So, don't mind your bleedin' clothes man. Clothes don't make you – *you* make you.'

'I just sometimes feel like I'm not good enough man, ya know?' I say through my tears.

'Martin?' starts Andy, 'you are *more* than enough man. And see your family? See your da, and Amy and Peter? In their eyes, you are a superhero. The people who love ya won't give a shite about your clothes, and the people that *do* have an opinion on what you're wearing? They're not your real friends, so why care what they think?'

Wow ... I'll tell you, for a sixteen-year-old, Andy speaks some sense. And his words have imprinted themselves onto my brain. I thank him from the bottom of my heart, and as we continue walking, we look over to see Tommy standing on his own.

'Here,' I say, 'come on, let's head over to Tommy. Maybe he needs to hear your words too man.'

And that's just what we did. At first, poor Tommy looked like he thought we were going to hit him, but when Andy gives his talk about what's really important, about friendship and not judging people, Tommy relaxes. Maybe Tommy needs someone to talk to too, ya know?

At home later that evening I'm in the kitchen making my dad a rasher and sausage sandwich – his favourite. I hear him come through our front door, and as he enters the kitchen and sees the sandwich and steaming hot cup of tea, he smiles and says, 'How much are ya looking for, eh? What is it you're looking for Martin?'

We both laugh as I say, 'I just want ya to know how much we appreciate you da.' I think we were both about to cry, so I made my excuses and headed up to my room. And as I walked in and caught sight of myself in the mirror I thought, 'You have enough – you *are* enough.'

Discuss

◆ Can you understand Martin's worries?

◆ Do you think he handled the pressure of 'Casual Monday' well?

◆ How important are your family and friends?

◆ Is Tommy really 'the bad guy,' or is he someone who is misunderstood?

◆ Do you think Andy spoke the truth?

These are just some of the questions I came up with as I wrote this story for you. I'm sure you have many more, so please don't be afraid to ask them. Feel free to write down your thoughts on this chapter in the Personal Reflections section at the back of this book.

If you feel like you can relate in any way to Martin, if you feel like you're not good enough, or your clothes are not as nice or as 'cool' as others, stop for a second and think this: Since when have clothes made any difference to the type of person you are? When you first came into the world, you were naked! Clothes and material things will never make you, you make you. So, always be proud of you.

And if you happen to be fortunate like Tommy and have the things you need, be sure you don't look down at those who don't. Be grateful for all you have, but don't think it somehow makes you special.

2.

'Sure, All Your Friends Are Doing It ...'

– Megan's Story

This has been the longest week – *ever*. Ever since Ciara told me she got us tickets for the Junior Cert party in Space nightclub in town, I have been unable to think of anything else. But the wait is finally over. It's Friday morning and I'm on my way to 'Curl-up and Dye' to get my hair and nails done. *'I'm gonna look massive,'* I laugh to myself as I sit on the bus and scroll through Snapchat. God ... I've just seen a video Vicky put up from last night. She looked drunk, like! What if her mam caught her? She is acting the muppet, although I do like Vicky. She kinda does whatever she wants, which I suppose is kinda cool.

I'm sitting in the chair in the salon listening to all the ladies as they have a gossip. My mam is the queen of gossiping, and this is pointed out to me by Mrs. O'Shay as she catches sight of me just before she is placed under a drier. 'Oh, heya Megan,' she says, 'how's your mam? Ohhh, she loves a good gossip your mam doesn't she?'

17

Both myself and Mrs. O'Shay share a laugh at my poor mam's expense. I like Mrs. O'Shay, as does my mam. She lives on her own and has no kids, but she is so good and so cool to all my friends and me. She is a plump lady, and I don't mean to slag her by saying that. It actually kinda makes her even more lovable.

'So, why are you getting all dolled up then Megan, eh?' enquires Mrs. O'Shay.

'I'm off to Space nightclub in town later Mrs. O'Shay. It's Junior Cert night.'

'Ah, I see. And look at the smile on your face. It's nearly as bright as your beautiful new blonde hair,' laughs Mrs. O'Shay, followed by, 'but Junior Cert night? Ah now, it can get a bit messy Megan – young ones drinking and what have ya. That won't be you now pet, sure it won't?'

I can actually see the concern etched on Mrs. O'Shay's face. 'Ah no Mrs. O' Shay, sure you know me. Good as gold so I am.'

'Ah, I know you are pet,' starts Mrs. O'Shay, 'just enjoy yourself and stay safe. That's the main thing.'

Back home and I'm up in my room applying the finishing touches. I've got Bruno Mars singing to me, as I look into the mirror which hangs on the back of my bedroom door. Hair? Done. Nails? Done. Me looking massive? Done! I laugh to myself at this last statement. It kinda feels weird to say good things about yourself sometimes, but my dad always says, *'If you don't love yourself, how can anyone else love you?'* So, although I'm not a diva or anything like that, I am proud of my reflection in the mirror. Besides, my hair and nails cost a bloody fortune, so I'd wanna look good!

Ah, my song has just come on the radio. Well, I say it's my song, but I haven't got a clue what it's called. It has a great beat, but I just love this next bit... *'I, I, follow, I follow you, Deep sea baby, I follow you...'* Tonight is going to be epic.

My phone lets off a beep to inform me I've got a new Whatsapp, and when I pick up my phone I see it's from Ciara. Ciara is my 'sister from another mister'. We are sooo close. I feel I can tell her anything, and I hope she feels the same. Ciara is really tall, and sometimes some of the meaner girls can poke fun at her. This really upsets me, but Ciara always handles it great. She just laughs it off and says, 'Ya hate me, cuz ya ain't me!' But, I know it gets to her sometimes, so I always make sure she knows I'm here.

'Hey Meg. So ru ready r wat? #juniornight #gonnabeepic,' reads Ciara's text.

'Lol. Leaving now xx,' comes my short reply.

Gosh. I can actually feel butterflies in my stomach. I can't wait to see the girls, to dance and dance and dance. And who knows? Maybe Robbie will be there too. He is only gorgeous! Captain of the school's GAA team, really smart, really funny, really kind, really gorgeous! Brown hair, green eyes, although, his teeth are blinding sometimes, kinda like Simon Cowell's! Still, as my mam says, *'No man is perfect Meg – except for your dad.'* Cringe!

Yep, I'd marry Robbie in a heartbeat – but I'd *never* tell him that. #morto.

I'm summoned into the kitchen by my mam, who seems to have invited the whole feckin' road into our house. When I enter I am met with, 'Ah would you look at this vision? My baby. Doesn't she look amazing?'

The whole kitchen chimes in with, 'yes she does.' I'm slightly mortified, but at the same time, it's really nice to hear nice things about yourself. So, I smile and thank everyone.

'Ah Trish, she's so good your Megan,' says our neighbour, Mrs. Burke, to my mam.

'And good is how she shall remain tonight, isn't that right Meg?' My mam has a way of making a statement sound like a bloody threat sometimes.

I laugh and reply, 'You have no need to worry mam.' And I truly meant that.

Soon I hear the beeping of a car and when I look out I see Ciara's dad has pulled up, with Ciara waving frantically out of the passenger window. She looks great, but then she always does. I say my goodbyes and as I'm heading out the door, my dad links my arm and walks me to the car, and as he does he says to me, 'If you don't want to do something, you just say?'

'No,' I reply.

'Just because your friends might want to do something, doesn't mean you have to,' continues my dad. 'What have I always taught you?'

God! I feel like I'm in school here with all the questions, but I know he is only worried about me, so I answer, 'Be a wolf, not a sheep. Be a leader, not a follower.'

'That's my girl. You know myself and your mam worry – it's kinda part of our job – but we really want you to have a ball, so make sure you do.'

'I will dad. Thank you. I love you so much.'

Ciara's dad drops us right outside Space nightclub, and we can see the queue is already huge. We say our goodbyes and listen to the last of the warnings coming from Ciara's dad. We are both so lucky to have such caring, yet cool dads. It's not long before we hear the scream of Sharon's voice.

'Ahhh girls!! It's about bloody time! *I've gotta feelin', that tonight's gonna be a good night...'*

Sharon has begun singing the Black Eyed Peas' classic as she holds out her arms and embraces us in a bear hug. Sharon is so funny, but she can be so wild too. She is a beautiful girl, with fire-red hair and a huge smile. I know I shouldn't, but I sometimes feel sorry for Sharon. She is the middle child of six, and can sometimes feel left out. Of course her mam and dad love her, but unfortunately they don't love each other anymore. Sharon's dad moved out a few months back, and although Sharon is putting on a brave face, both myself and Ciara know deep down she is hurting. So, we do all we can to keep our eye on her.

'C'mon, we're all over here,' starts Sharon, 'and we're drinkin' a load of beer!' Sharon begins laughing at her own rhyme. 'Well, look at that girls. I'm a poet and I didn't know it!' I look at Ciara and as our eyes meet, I can tell she is thinking what I am – Sharon is drunk.

It's not long before Sharon brings us to the part of the queue where the rest of the girls are. And standing right in the middle of the group is Vicky, as she holds everyone's attention with one of her mad stories. This group consists of six girls, including Vicky and Sharon, and all the group seem to holding plastic 7-up bottles. 'Howya Meg, howya Ciara. Great to see ya's.' Vicky kinda slurs these words towards us, then proceeds to launch her arms around us both and hold us in two bloody headlocks! Again, it's clear to see that Vicky is drunk too. I personally don't get it. Like, I understand why girls and boys my age start to drink – actually, no I don't get it. I don't agree with it at all.

Don't get me wrong, I'm far from a goody-two-shoes, just ask my mam! But I am strong-minded. I am not a sheep.

'Where's your drink girls?' asks Vicky.

Ciara answers first. 'Eh, we don't have any, and won't be having any either.'

'Damn straight,' I add.

'Ahh yiz'er dry auld shites aren't ya's?' laughs Vicky. We both know she means no harm and is only slagging us.

'Sure, all your friends are doing it,' says Sharon to us both. 'Come *onn*, I promise not to tell your mammy or daddy.' Sharon turns to the girls and rolls her eyes to heaven as she makes this statement. It's not like Sharon to be so rude.

I take her to one side and I say, 'Shar, are you okay? This isn't like you. You don't have to drink to have a great night you know.'

'Ahh feck off Meg. Just cuz you're a lightweight, don't go tryin' to make...' Sharon doesn't make it to the end of this statement, as she trips over herself. I catch her just in time. 'I'm grand – leave me alone, yeah?' Sharon almost barks this at me. She has never spoken to me like that before. I walk away feeling upset.

Somehow, the girls who are drinking find enough composure to keep it together as they are met at the club's door by the bouncers. There are no signs of any 7-up bottles, so we can only assume they drank every last drop. Great!

As we walk in, the bass hits us in the stomach, as my song blares from the massive speakers on the stage. *'I, I follow, I follow you, Deep Sea Baby, I follow you...'*

Myself and Ciara are about to head to the dance floor, when Vicky grabs us. 'Look what I snuck in.' She opens her bag to reveal a naggin of vodka. 'Are you sure you won't join me girls?' enquires Vicky, her words becoming more slurred.

'You're grand thanks,' replies Ciara as we both make our way to the dance floor.

'He's right behind you,' says Ciara, and when I turn to see Robbie dancing with his mates I feckin' freeze. 'Just say howya,' continues Ciara.

I don't know where I got the courage from, but suddenly I find myself right in front of Robbie, smiling like a big eejit – and he's smiling back! #dreamy

'Are ya having a good night?' he asks.

'It's deadly,' I reply. 'Are you drinking and all?' I enquire.

'No way,' starts Robbie, 'I have a match tomorrow, so I don't want a hangover you know?' He winks as he says this, and then says, 'like, I do drink an' all, sometimes.'

'I think it's really cool that you're not drinking actually,' I say, 'we have a whole life of being adults waiting for us. For me? That's when I want to start drinking. For now? I just wanna be a teenager and do teenage stuff.' God! I hope I don't sound like a fool. But Robbie's answer informs me I don't.

'That is so true, and kinda deadly. I love that Meg. You're really cool, do you know that?' I blush, turn to Ciara, and just smile.

I spent the rest of the night on the dance floor with Ciara, Robbie and Mick. Ciara really likes Mick, and we think he likes her too – you know what boys are like. Suddenly, I feel a wave of guilt. I was having so much fun, I haven't thought once about Sharon, Vicky, and all the girls who are drinking. I see Rita, a girl we all know, and ask has she seen any of the girls.

'Oh, I saw them alright. They got thrown out by the bouncers, *whilst getting sick*, and the bouncers had to take one of their phones and call their dad. I think it was Vicky's dad who came, and let's just say, he's not too happy. Sharon was sobbing, god love her. It just doesn't seem worth it, Meg, does it?'

'No,' I think to myself, *'it's really not worth it.'*

Two days later and my phone rings. It's Sharon. 'Heya hun,' she starts, 'c'mere, was I rude to you the other night?'

I think for a split second about my answer. Truthfully? Sharon was a little rude. But does she need to hear that now? I think she does actually. I will give her a piece of my mind, but I won't stay mad at her. I do love Sharon after all. 'You were drunk, Shar, and not very nice to me. I'm just not into all that drinking an' all Sharon, and I don't think it suits you either.'

'Ah Jesus Meg, what was I thinking. It's not like me at all, but Vicky was like, *'ahh go on, sure we're all doin' it. Don't be such a loser Shar',* and like a sap I did. I'm now grounded, and I've upset you Meg, which is killing me. I've no phone for two months, as you can tell cuz I'm ringing ya on the house phone, but worst of all? My mam and dad feel so let down.'

'They'll come around,' I reassure her.

'I should've done what your da always says to do – what is it again, Meg?' ask Sharon.

I smile as I reply, 'Be a wolf, not a sheep – be a leader, not a follower.'

'That's what I should've done,' starts Sharon, 'there is plenty of time for me to find out about alcohol and what suits me. Anyway, what are you up to Meg?'

Again, I feel a smile begin to form, and this is one smile I have no control over. 'I'm heading to the pictures in an hour with Robbie...'

Great night? Check. No alcohol needed? Check. Get a date with Robbie – *check*.

Be a wolf, not a sheep – be a leader, not a follower.

Discuss

◆ Is Meg a 'lightweight?'

◆ Is alcohol, or any type of substance, needed to have a good time?

◆ Why do you think Sharon gave in to peer pressure?

◆ Could there be a reason for Vicky being a little wild?

◆ What would you do?

These are just some of the questions I came up with as I wrote this story for you. I'm sure you have many more, so please don't be afraid to ask them. Feel free to write down your thoughts on this chapter in the Personal Reflections section at the back of this book.

I want to share something with you here. I am a recovering alcoholic. I am proud to tell you that, at the time of writing, I am over four years sober. 'Ahh, so you hate "the drink," and that's why you wrote this chapter,' you might think. Nothing could be further from the truth. The truth is that alcohol can be dangerous when it is abused. I was a bit like 'Sharon' in this story when I was younger. I only began drinking because 'everyone else was doing it'. If I had a time-machine, I'd go back to fourteen-year-old Gary and say, 'Snap out of it ya sap! Be a wolf, not a sheep.'

Legally, you cannot drink until you are eighteen, so my advice is to wait until then.

If you are reading this and feel like you may have issues with drinking, please don't be afraid to tell your folks, your extended family, your friends and so on. They may get upset with you at first and be disappointed, but you can bet they will do everything they can to help you.

3.

'The Importance of Family and Friends' – Doug and Josh's Story

Doug: Hi there. My name is Doug, and I'm here to have an auld chat with you. A chat that might make you cringe a little when you hear me use words like, *'I love him/her sooo much'* or, *'I don't know what I'd do without them.'*

But I really hope our little chat makes you think.

I live in a cool town called Ballymahon in County Longford. It's a small town filled with great people. I am about half-way through sixth year – the most stressful feckin' year of all – and I am here to tell you that without the support of my family and friends I don't know where my head would be at. So, that's what I'd like to talk to you about – family, friends, and how important it is to talk about how you might be feeling. I'm so lucky, as I have my full family all around me. Mam, dad, two sisters, two aunts and two uncles. But I am fully aware not everyone has the same luck. In fact, I have asked my best friend, Josh, to help me out with this chat, as sadly Josh isn't as lucky as I am. I'll let Josh explain.

Josh: Cheers Doug. My name is Josh, and like Doug, I too live in Ballymahon. We are a little different to other lads our age. I don't know when or how it started, but we have always been really comfortable talking about *anything* to each other. Almost six years ago, my dad was killed in a road accident. Nobody was at fault, but that doesn't make things any easier. I took it bad. I am the eldest of three boys, and I was super-close to my dad. I'm not for a minute saying I miss him more or the most – I just really miss him. We talked about everything – he was my hero. Yes, after he died, I became very angry and cut myself off from everyone, but I could see how much that was upsetting my mam. So, I asked for help. I went to see a counsellor and it was the best decision I ever made. Today? Today I still miss dad with all my heart – we all do. But as a family we have grown closer together. I am also very lucky as I have the best mates a lad could ask for, like auld Doug here.

Doug: Ahh nice one Josh, you're too kind! Right, shall we get started?

So, you know the way, nowadays, everyone is banging on about, *'It's so important to talk,'* or, *'It's okay not to be okay.'* We hear these statements so often that they can begin to lose their value. So, I ask you, the person reading this, when was the last time you stopped and actually pondered those statements. *'It's so important to talk'* or *'It's okay not to be okay.'* Let's start with the second one first shall we? Confused? Good. *'It's okay not to be okay.'* Pretty straight forward right? There is nothing wrong with feeling sad, upset, scared, worried, stressed. None of these are nice feelings to experience, but it doesn't make you a weirdo if you feel them. My first experience of knowing that 'it's okay not to be okay' might make you laugh.

Right, well, I wasn't at *all* okay when Pauly Dunne was picked to be captain of our local GAA team. I wasn't okay in the feckin' slightest! I got moody. I was a nightmare to be around. I didn't take the news well at all. And then? Then I started feeling guilty. Why? Because I really like Pauly Dunne – he's sound. So why was I not okay? Enter my uncle Noel, 'The Fountain of Knowledge.'

'It's okay that you're feeling this way Douggie. It's natural. The trick is not to unpack your bags and live in that negativity forever. Talk about how you feel. You can talk to me, your manager, even Pauly Dunne. Don't feel embarrassed. And remember, there is actually a good side to you not feeling okay too buddy. You will learn from this. It will drive you on, to help you learn how to deal with difficult situations, especially ones that don't go your way. But for now? It's okay not to be okay about it.'

There you have it folks. My uncle Noel made me realise that my feelings of 'not being okay' about the situation with Pauly was actually disappointment and not resentment. And these words from my uncle Noel also show just how important it is to open up and share our feelings. What do you think Josh?

Josh: I couldn't agree more, but I'm going to save my opinion on these two matters for later if that's okay? Gary has asked me to talk to you all in another chapter, so I'll discuss *'It's so important to talk,'* and, *'It's okay not to be okay,'* in that chapter. But for now? I couldn't agree with you more Doug.

What I *would* like to talk to you all about is the importance of your family and friends. Me? I would literally be lost without them. I know this might sound – I dunno – strange, but I kinda feel I had to 'grow up fast' after my dad died. I am the eldest and I suppose I put a lot of pressure on my own shoulders. I was worried about mam, worried about my brothers, and I forgot to worry about myself. But I had you Josh. And when I think back to the support you and others gave me? Well, it's why I'm in a much better place. I suppose, at the start, I was too embarrassed to express my true feelings. I felt like a 'sap' for crying, like an eejit for being upset. But as soon as I talked about how I was feeling, you all rallied around me. You all made me see that it is actually foolish *not* to talk.

Doug: Wow Josh that is so nice to hear. But, and I hope you don't mind me saying this, I think we all did something else for you too. I think we got you to see how important your family is too.

Josh: Yes you did. At the time I had actually fooled myself into thinking that I couldn't talk to my family at all. Sure, I'll let you explain what happened next, Doug.

Doug: Look, Josh's situation is just shit. There is no denying that. Yes, we did all we could to support him, but I remember thinking to myself one day that he was pushing his family away, so I intervened. I was shitting myself that day, if you remember Josh? I didn't want to come across like, 'my dad is incredible and I tell him everything and I'd be lost without him...' I just wanted you to know that you still had family members who would walk across hot coals for you, like your mam, your uncles, and all your cousins, not to mention your two brothers. Families can offer us a different kind of support than our friends.

Josh: I suppose, in my defense, I didn't want to upset them. They had lost a husband, a brother a dad too, ya know? Still, I'm so glad you had that talk with me that day.

Doug: So, there ya have it folks. There are our opinions, for what they're worth, on the importance of family and friends in your life. Today's world sees all different types of families. Some parents don't stay together as a couple. Sometimes mam or dad might find someone new, and the 'family dynamic' changes. But at the heart of it all is the core of your family – mam and dad, aunts, uncles, cousins, etc. So, if you need them? Use them. And the same goes for your friends too. Don't feel embarrassed or foolish for telling your friend that you're not okay. Talk ... share ... express. That's what friends are for.

Discuss

♦ Do you feel silly telling those closest to you how you feel?

♦ Do you sometimes shut your family out because 'they wouldn't understand'?

♦ Was Doug over the top for being so upset about not being picked as the captain of the GAA team?

♦ Did Josh do the right thing by not telling his family how he feels because he 'didn't want to upset them?'

♦ Do me a favour will you? Pick up your phone and send your best friend a text saying, 'I'm so glad you're in my life, and I hope I'm as good a friend to you as you are to me.' After you hit send, go up to a member of your family – any of them – and just give them an auld hug. Why? Because deep down, you know it's the right thing to do.

These are just some of the questions I came up with as I wrote this story for you. I'm sure you have many more, so please don't be afraid to ask them. Feel free to write down your thoughts on this chapter in the Personal Reflections section at the back of this book.

So there you have it – my take on how important both friends and family can be in your life. Yes, I'm sure they can do your head in sometimes, but then, I bet you do theirs in sometimes too! And as you go through life, remember this: It's not just about what your family and friends do for you. It's equally about what you do for them.

And remember: never, ever, be afraid to talk.

4.

(Un)Social Media

In this chapter we take a break from our case studies and instead focus on different aspects of a topic that is close to my heart when it comes to young people: social media. I'm hoping that it might get you to think about, and approach using, apps like Facebook, Instagram and Snapchat, among others, in a more positive and less harmful way.

If I was to start slating social media in its entirety, I would most likely come across as some kind of 'aul' fella' who doesn't have a clue. So I won't do that, and besides I *love* social media myself. On the other hand, there seems to be massive pressure and strife for young people as soon as they set up a Snapchat account or make a new page on Facebook. So let's look at five elements to the unsocial side of social media that I find worrying. I settled on these five as they seemed to be the most common problems that have come up when I am talking to students. First up, cyberbullying/trolling.

(1) Cyberbullying/Trolling

I'm sure you will agree that this one is a no-brainer. If we went back twenty-five years ago to when I was fifteen we would see that I was bullied as a kid. It was horrible. I was different. I had long hair, which I had shaved underneath. I was a 'heavy metaller' and loved bands like Guns 'N' Roses, Pantera, and Metallica. All of which were enough to make me a target. But that is all a bully needs sometimes – for you to be a little 'different'. I would get chased home from school, but as soon as I got to the front door of my home, as soon as I saw my mam, I could relax. Why? Because the bully was *outside* my home. He couldn't get near me. He couldn't call me all the names he just *loved* to call me. I was safe in the comfort of my home. But today? Today it's different.

Picture this. A young girl or boy, who is currently being trolled and/or bullied online, comes home from school.

'Heya mam, what's for dinner?'

'Ah heya pet. It's stew, but it won't be ready for another twenty minutes or so. How was your day? Is everything good?'

It is at this point that the young girl or boy might lie. Maybe it's embarrassment? Maybe they don't want to worry their folks? Or maybe they are just afraid of the bully. All I know is, when you are being bullied, you often don't think straight. 'I'm grand mam. Great day today. I'll head up to my room. Give me a shout when dinner is ready. I love your stew mam.' And off they go to their room.

But here's the thing. As soon as they close their bedroom door behind them and pull out their smartphone or laptop and log into the app they are being bullied on, whether it be Facebook, Snapchat or something else, it's like they are opening their bedroom door and saying to the bully, 'Come on in ... *make yourself at home while you bully the shite out of me.*' This is a real worry. We can all agree that bullying is vile, but before social media it could only be done face to face. But today, these bullies can now remain anonymous and it is this anonymity provided by social media that can be used by these cowards – because that's what they are guys, *cowards* – to gain someone's trust and then terrorise them in front of their friends. And it may shock you to know that there are countless adults also being bullied in this manner – *every* day.

So, I think we need to get tough. We need to eradicate this bullshit once and for all. Do we fight back? We could, I suppose, but you will never win with a bully so I don't recommend it. Do we do the same to them? *Never.* Don't ever sink to their level, never lower yourself to their sub-standards in any situation. My advice? *Block them*! And if you have to block them everyday? *Then block them every feckin' day*. You shouldn't have to do this – it's shitty, I know – but then, if we didn't have bullies in the first place...

Sadly, we do. So I highly advise you to block them. And here is why:

They have absolutely nothing good to say, feel or think about you. If you were sitting in a room and someone kept calling you names, you would more than likely get up and leave. You know it's wrong, and you don't need to hear it. So blocking some fool who wants to run you down is the same as getting up and leaving that room. Does blocking someone make you weak, a coward, a gobshite? *No way!* Blocking someone who is talking crap about you makes you the smartest person I know. And if after blocking them, they keep it up? Take screenshots of their bullshit and show it to an adult you trust. And, most importantly, if you are being attacked online, make sure to tell as many of your friends and family as possible, and allow them to help you in any way they can.

Remember, it's not you that has the problem – it's them!

But what if the bullying or trolling is being done by someone you know personally? What if you and this person share online friends? Blocking them from your page, won't stop your mutual friends from seeing what this moron has to say about you if they post their bullshit on their own page or timeline. That makes things slightly more difficult to deal with – or does it?

Firstly, let's say this person has just put up some lies about you, or has started to slag you on their own page on Facebook. You have the ability and the right to report the post, and you can cite that you feel you are being bullied/ trolled as a result of it. Again, this is not 'ratting' or 'telling tales,' and it is most-certainly not a sign of weakness. You never asked to be in this position, so all you are doing is what you can to stomp out this bullshit.

Once you do that, you could then put up a post of your own. This is something I had to do not long after my first book came out. I was being trolled on a regular basis, but one moron went too far. So I reported their bullshit, and then put up a post explaining what I had done and why. I didn't 'name and shame' this idiot in my post. I didn't resort to calling him names, or slagging him off. That is something he would do – and I'm a much better person than he is. I simply put up this post, so that my true friends knew what I was dealing with. And those who still chose to believe what this person had to say about me after reading my post? Well, good riddance! I don't need people like that in my life so 'see ya later'. And to me, that is the key in this situation. Your true friends, the ones who always have your back, will never believe the bullshit of some cyberbully or troll.

Throughout this book I will be encouraging you to talk to as many people as you can about how you feel and how you are doing. So, if you feel you have to put up a post like the above, try first going to your folks, your brother or sister, your aunty or uncle, your teacher or whomever you trust, and ask them for guidance. Tell them what you have gone through with this cyberbully/troll. Tell this adult that you have blocked this idiot, but they are still posting about you on their own page. Explain that you want to put up a short post of your own to debunk their lies about you, then allow this adult to assist you in constructing this post. And remember, your true friends will believe *you*.

I really wish we didn't have to have a discussion about *any* type of bullying, but sadly we do. So let's all join together and help each other out. Be mindful that some malevolent, mean-spirited people live on social media. They are cowards and losers, but they can do a lot of damage. So block them and be really proud of yourself for doing so.

(2) Negative Body Image

This one applies to young people in general, but sadly I think the young women of today are more likely to be affected by it. So, I hope I can throw some light on this for you.

When I was in college, many moons ago, I loved learning all about Graphic Design. We got introduced to Photoshop, and almost instantly my head was spinning. Guys, it is incredible how much you can alter a photo of someone through this software, and if you're good at it, no one would ever know. Our lecturer was a really cool guy and one day he gave the entire class a photo of his own wife so we could mess about and change her appearance. Of course we all had a laugh. I think I had her looking like Krusty the Clown from *The Simpsons* at one stage. But after the laughs came the serious bits. He was able to show us just how powerful this software really is. I couldn't believe it but you can literally make someone look exactly how you want them to.

Skip forward to today and Instagram. Great app, great for the craic and so on, but also full to the brim with barefaced liars! Why? Because trust me guys, s*ome* (not all) of the influencers you follow are either deadly at Photoshop themselves or they pay someone who is. And for the lads? Remember this ... the lighting in the room when you take a photo can change everything. I mean, when I walk into the bathroom with my top off in the morning, I give myself a fright and think, 'Jaysis, I need to get back to the gym'. Yet I can walk into the same jacks *that evening* when the lighting has changed and I'll be like, 'Well hellloooo, don't you look bleedin' deadly?' It's just the light lads – trust me.

But if we are body conscious, if we are already feeling a bit shitty about our weight, our hair, our biceps or whatever, and we try to measure ourselves off these 'picture perfect' models that adorn all platforms of social media, we will drive ourselves mad and end up with a really negative body image.

So, here again is my opinion on this matter – feck them! Seriously, lads and ladies, just feck them! Be happy with *you* and the body *you* have, and be happy for *them* and whatever they have going on. In fact, if you find that the only reason you are following *anyone* online is because of how they look, and not because of how they make you think or feel, then I'd personally stop following them. Only ever change your body for *you* or maybe for your health. Instead of envying other people's fake photos, put up your own photos of how you like to look and feel, and do so with pride.

One of the best decisions I made for myself since my release from prison was deciding to eat in a more healthy manner – well, kinda! I'm not saying I'll never eat McDonald's or crisps or ice cream again, that would be madness. I just truly believe that a healthy body leads to a healthy mind. But having a drop-dead perfect body is very difficult to achieve and may simply be unrealistic for many of us. So remember, if it's not your thing, don't beat yourself up about it.

The important thing is to not measure yourself against 'the beautiful people from social media'. In order for someone to love you, you've first got to love yourself. So be proud of you, your body, your mind, and your spirit. And always remember simply to be the best that you can be.

(3) The Human Connection

Right. Before you start yawning and thinking, *'Is this gonna be some hippy-I-love-everything speech now*

Gary?' open your mind and bear with me. As human beings, it is vital for us to be able to communicate and create real-life, personal connections with each other. And when you are in your teens, the process of meeting people and creating new friendships is not only important it can also be great craic. But it can be pretty hard to do all this 'connecting on a human level' when our heads are glued to the screens of our phones, looking at other people's lives. It's actually mad, isn't it? We sit there admiring other people's lives in some virtual world when we could go and *meet* the person and admire them to their face in the real one! Believe me, it's important to have human interaction guys.

Think of this: Have you ever had the chats with someone for *hours* online, then meet them later on and have feck all to say? You both just kinda stand there. If one of you actually *does* come up with something to say, you wish to yourself that you could reach into your pocket and pull out a massive emoji to show them how you feel! Mad isn't it?

It's like, the more social media sucks you in, the more *unsocial* you become ... and that applies to us all.

As an idea, how about giving yourself a 'detox' of sorts from social media? Yes, I'm sure your blood ran cold as you read those words, but hear me out, then see what you think.

If you take little breaks from social media, it can do wonders. I find I'm not always reaching for my phone to see if someone put up a picture of their dinner or something. And here's the thing. If you happen to feel you can relate to the previous two chapters, taking a break from social media will actually help you so much. 'Ah, but Gar me auld flower, I'd have massive FOMO (Fear of Missing Out)' I hear you say. Well, how about you and a group of your friends do this detox together? This will hopefully bring you all closer together too because if you want to chat, you will have to go and see the person. Maybe organise days out shopping in town, or arrange football matches in your local park. Then it will be *everyone else* with FOMO, as they are missing out on all the fun you're having.

And this detox doesn't have to be for a long period of time – just whatever is long enough for you. I do it all the time, and when I go back online, I appreciate it a whole lot more. Just something to think about.

(4) Privacy and 'Likes'

Having a bit of privacy these days can be difficult, right? We have embraced all types of social media with gusto, and as a result we get to see many aspects of people's lives. Holidays, weddings, birthdays, or even just a night out with friends can be documented in countless photos and videos and posted online for people to see. And we all do this – me included! But at the same time, having a bit of privacy in your life is vital. And if we are being really honest with ourselves, we usually post these pictures or videos in order to see how many 'likes' we get. I'll come back to that in a second, but before I do I want to try to explain my personal opinions on privacy.

When I was seventeen, my entire world collapsed. My beautiful daughter, Megan, passed away. It ripped me in half, and in many ways I am still suffering from her loss today. Megan was born in 1996 and died in 1997 – a time when there was little or no social media to be found. It was also a time when all your phone could do was make a call or text – how mental is that? Megan's mam and I wanted as many photos of our beautiful daughter as possible, so we bought a camera. We then took a ton of photos and left them in to get developed. I still have every single one of those photos today – but not one of them can be found anywhere online. Am I ashamed of Megan? Jesus no! I just feel that the moments we all shared are private, and it feels nice to know I can keep these moments to myself . In other words, I enjoy having some privacy in this situation.

Even in the age of social media though some aspects of your life should remain private to you. For example, let's say you've just shared your first kiss with you new boyfriend or girlfriend. That is a really special moment, right? So why put up a million photos and videos of it? It's really cool to keep some things to yourself. So always be mindful of your own privacy. Ask yourself, 'Do I really want everyone to see, or know, everything about this aspect of my life?'

But when it comes to social media, privacy has two serious sides to it that I want you to think about. Let me explain:

Let's say you and your family are heading away on your holidays for two weeks in the sun. You are super-excited and can't wait to post a picture from the airport with the caption, 'The whole family off for two weeks in the sun ... yeah!' We saw earlier that there are some evil idiots online, but there are also some opportunistic ones as well and you have now just told them that your house is empty for the next two weeks. If you really want to share this airport photo, just be mindful of who might see it. Or maybe don't say how long you will be away for, or add a little 'white lie' like, 'and a massive thank you to Aunty A and Uncle B for house-sitting for us'.

Unfortunately, this happened to a wonderful couple I know. They were heading away on their first family holiday with two young children so there was a big post telling all their friends about their upcoming adventures. But when they arrived home? Their house had been ransacked. It could be a massive coincidence, but why take that chance? So it might be a good idea to wait until you are home, and then share as many photos and videos as you like showing what an amazing time you had. Or, just keep the memories to yourself and within your family.

The second serious side to privacy online is unfortunate, but you need to think about it. Let's say you are on a night out, you've had a few drinks and are 'acting the maggot'. Posting drunk pictures of yourself online can seem like a 'bit of a laugh' at the time, but it might not be the best idea. Let's say you are going for a job interview, even some years later, and your prospective employers decide to take a look at your social media accounts to see what you are 'really like'. And if they come across an array of photos and videos of you drunk or worse, they may form a very different opinion of you. This may seem unfair, but it is sadly the world we live in.

On this year's *Love Island 2019*, one of the contestants was removed early from the show because of a tweet they posted almost a year before. From what I can gather, this tweet was deemed racist so the show's producers immediately removed this person from the show. The moral of the story: be very careful what you post online.

So privacy is something you need to take seriously. But why do we post pictures and posts in the first place – and let's be honest here. Most people do it for 'likes', and I think this is just a load of crap. 'Likes' don't mean shit guys. Honestly. 'Likes' are just a snapshot of a moment in time. Did you know that there are companies out there who study social media to come up with the best times of the day to put up a post or picture to ensure you get the most likes possible? What a load of unnecessary crap! Just because your photo or your post didn't get as many 'likes' as 'Mary's' or 'Johnny's' doesn't mean a thing. It really doesn't. You should never feel like you are in a competition with anyone online, especially not for feckin' 'likes!'

Instagram has recently done an incredible thing. They have removed the ability for others to see how many likes a person got on their post. Only the person who posted it can see how many likes they got – and they are the only ones who should matter in this situation. So please, try with all your might not to get caught up in all the 'how many likes did I get' stuff. It's not a competition, and should never be treated as one.

(5) Online Safety

Now not for one second do I think that you, the reader, is an eejit! So please accept my apologies in advance if you think this section is insulting your intelligence. I just have to make clear something you are likely already aware of, which is that there are serious dangers lurking online.

Lets start with the basics. Never, ever, give your personal details, especially your bank details, to anyone you don't trust. If you are doing some online shopping and you're not sure if the site you are on 'feels right', ask an adult to have a glance over it and they can help you make your decision. And if you get emails or texts telling you that you have just won something like loads of money or a new car, ask yourself, 'Did I enter a competition to win money or a new car?' If you didn't enter a competition, you can't be the winner, so chances are the text or email you received is a scam. And sadly, there are thousands of scams online so you have to be vigilant.

Another very dangerous aspect to online safety is meeting up with someone you have only chatted to online – especially if none of these chats were video chats. Look, we've all seen the MTV show *Catfish*, so we know how crazy meeting up in person with someone you have only chatted to through text can be. It may not be the girl or boy in the picture on their profile and, more importantly, they may have something sinister in mind for you. The risk is way too high, so please, never, meet up with someone in person until you have spent a long time getting to know them and have shared video chats together. And even then? Bring people with you to the first few meetings – just in case. Keep your wits about you at all times.

The last dangerous aspect to online safety I want to discuss has sadly happened to many young men and women the world over. Have you ever been asked to send or share nude or almost nude photos of yourself? If you have, I am so sorry you had to go through that and please know that it is never okay. It may seem exciting at the time, but you never know where those photos will end up. Even worse, sometimes criminals want these pictures in order to try to blackmail you. If anyone, and I mean anyone, asks you to send them pictures that you are not comfortable with, tell them to take a long walk off a short pier – in other words, say, '*absolutley not*'. Even if you are in a relationship with this person, the risk is too high. If they try to tell you that you're a 'chicken' or that 'so and so does it all the time', again tell them to take a hike! Always know your self-worth.

So that brings to an end this chapter on *some* of the negative sides to social media. Young people are under a lot of pressure these days and, unfortunately, many of those pressures can be found on social media. So get strong and get smart. Nobody is saying burn your smartphone or never use the internet again. Just be mindful that, like in real life, there are some very unpleasant people online.

Discuss

♦ Is cyberbullying a problem in your life? If so, please don't try to 'go it alone.' Don't feel stupid, silly, or weak. Be strong and tell someone ... talk to someone. It is not your fault.

♦ Are there any more negative sides to social media that affect you? Start a conversation about them at home, or in your school. Remember the line from before – *be a leader, not a follower.*

These are just some of the questions I came up with as I wrote this chapter for you. I'm sure you have many more, so please don't be afraid to ask them. Feel free to write down your thoughts on this chapter in the Personal Reflections section at the back of this book.

5.

'It's Just Not Worth It'
– Jimmy's Story

'Ah man. Last Saturday night was unreal, Jimmy.' I am getting the low-down from my friend Simon on the antics of last Saturday night. I had a family dinner to go to, so I couldn't join Simon, the lads, and more importantly, the ladies, as they all went to Sandra's for a house party. *#massiveFOMO.*

Sandra's folks are away on holiday, so it's 'free gaff central' in Sandra's.

'No way Simon yeah? Was it that good?'

'I'm not gonna lie to ya Jimmy – it *really* was!' Simon squints his green eyes, and puts a ton of emphasis on the word 'really,' just to add effect. I'm close to Simon, but he scares me sometimes. He just has that whole 'I don't give a crap' attitude. Some find this cool, but I personally think it's a bit manic. Still, he is my mate, and I've always got his back. He is a short guy for his age (just turned eighteen) with mousey-brown hair, and what looks like bum-fluff on his face. God love him, he thinks it's a beard! Still, who am

I to slag? My hair is so blonde, I almost look like an albino. And if I attempt to grow facial hair? Let's just say it doesn't work out.

'I got a snog off April too man,' says Simon proudly.

'What?!?' I say surprised, 'No way! How did you manage that? I mean, no offence pal, but you're punching above your weight there aren't ya?' I lightly and playfully tickle Simon just under his ribs.

'Give it over ya sap,' he laughs. 'And while I'm at it,' he continues, 'don't hate the player man – hate the game.' This statement unites us both in laughter. 'And guess who was asking for you Jimmy? None other than the beautiful Sarah.'

I stop dead on the footpath. 'Don't be acting the maggot here now Simon. Don't take the piss man.' I can actually feel my heart pick up its pace. Sarah is just – wow! Dark hair, amazing eyes. I mean, she is kinda perfect. 'What did she say Simon, and leave nothing out!'

Simon laughs as he says, 'Well, she came up to me and was like, *'Where's Jimmy. I was really hoping he'd be here,'* and I was like, *'Ah he was gonna come, but then he decided to stay at home and help his nana finish knitting a jumper.'* She didn't seem too impressed man.'

My face changes from a smile to a scowl. 'Feck off you ya mad yoke. You better not have said that,' I say.

'I'm only buzzin' ya mad thing. Don't worry, I put in a good word for ya. Besides, you'll get your chance to dazzle her with your charm tonight at Sandra's. Her folks are home in two days, so tonight is our last free gaff. It's gonna be deadly man.'

I allow myself to let Simon's words sink in. He's right – tonight is going to be *deadly!*

We make it back to mine, and after a quick chat with my mam we head up to my room to begin making ourselves look like two male models. 'So, have you got your drink boxed off Jimmy, yeah?'

'I do, I do indeed,' comes my reply.

'Deadly man,' starts Simon, 'and I'm after getting us both a bag of Patsy too.'

'Patsy?' I ask bewildered.

'Patsy Cline is slang for a line, you know, a line of coke.'

My face changes. 'Coke? As in, cocaine?' I can't hide the worry in my voice.

'Ahh Jimmy I'm tellin' ya, it's deadly man. It gives you this confidence and makes ya feel like ya can do anything. Don't be worrying man.'

'I'm not worried,' I lie. Truth be known? I was shitting. But feck it. I'm sure it will be grand. 'How the hell did you get this Patsy anyway?' I ask.

'Off the boys down at the shops. I got them on tick too, so I don't even have to pay for them until next week. And don't worry man, this one is on me.' Simon reaches into his Man. United wallet and takes out two tiny plastic bags filled with a white powder. 'We'll do a quick one now to get the buzz going,' smiles Simon.

What am I doing? Ahh, I'm sure I will be fine. Won't I?

We're heading to Sandra's and my heart feels like it's going to jump right out of my chest. But this is not brought on by how nervous I am about seeing Sarah, it is being brought on by the effects of cocaine. I'm not sure if I like it, but one thing I do know is myself and Jimmy have not shut up talking to each other! It's like we're both trying to interrupt each other as we speak.

'Ya alright man?' asks Simon.

'Yeah man, like, I'm buzzin' and all. Just not sure if I like it to be honest.'

'I was like that too when I did my first few lines. You'll get the hang of it pal. And if ya don't like it? Just give the bag to me and I'll polish it off.'

'I'm sure I'll be grand man,' I lie.

As we walk up the driveway of Sandra's, we can hear the music coming from her back garden. The evening's summer sun is slowly beginning it's descent, and I'm feeling kinda euphoric. But I am also sweating like mad, and for some reason, I seem to have lost the control of the lower part of my jaw! I look over at Simon and I don't really recognise him. He has been dipping into his 'bag of Patsy' all the way here, and he just looks out of it. We both walk into Sandra's and head straight out to the back garden. All the lads and ladies seem to be here. April sees Simon and makes a beeline for him, and after a quick hello, Simon just kinda kisses her. I've *never* seen him so confident. But then, I see him slip his bag of coke to April, and I watch as she disappears into the downstairs toilet. This all feels a bit strange, but feck it. I don't want to be a dry-shite. Besides, maybe I will get the same confidence when I see Sarah. Maybe she likes to do coke too.

I didn't have to wait too long to find out. Sarah and I kinda bump into each other at the sink in Sandra's kitchen. 'Hi Jimmy, you look great,' says Sarah.

My insides feel like they are in a washing machine at full spin. 'You look, eh, great your, eh, self Sarah yeah?' I can actually feel the sweat at the top of my forehead.

'Thanks Jimmy,' starts Sarah followed by, 'are you okay? Like, you're sweating. And what's up with your jaw?'

'I'm after doin' a few lines of coke Sarah. Do you want some?' Sarah's smile has been replaced by a look of total disgust. 'Eh, *no thanks, and no way*. And I'm super-surprised that you are doing it too Jimmy. What's the big attraction? April is doing it, as is Mary and Annie too, not to mention some of the lads. Me? I think it's disgusting, and it is actually ruining people's lives these days.'

I feel like utter crap as Sarah speaks to me. She is, of course, completely right. Why in god's name did I try this crap in the first place? Listening to Sarah is making me realise that I have hated every moment since I put this white shite up my nose. I'm not sure if it's the coke or my true fears, but suddenly I find myself crying – in front of Sarah. 'What am I after doing Sarah? Like, Jesus. You know me. I hate all the peer pressure shite. Sarah, I am out of it right now, and I don't like it one bit.'

Just as I admit this to Sarah, we both turn to see Simon and April dancing like lunatics in the middle of the garden, while everyone stands around cheering and laughing.

'April is really cool, Jimmy, but lately she has been doing a lot of that coke crap. She tells me it gives her confidence. I told her that's bullshit, that she doesn't need a disgusting drug to feel good about herself. But, of course, I was just called a wet-blanket and told to mind my own business. It's sad Jimmy, because away from the coke? She is a really nice girl.'

'Simon is the same,' I say, noting that I feel rushes running throughout my body as I talk. I really don't like this feeling. 'He told me this stuff makes you feel like you can do anything, and yet I've done it, and now I can barely talk to you. I'm scared too Sarah.' And I truly was scared. I've gone out drinking in the past, and although I know I was too young, I could *kind of* handle it. But this? This is madness. Simon looks like he's having a ball, which scares me even more.

'Come on,' says Sarah, 'let's get out of here.' You can come over to my house. My eldest brother and his girlfriend are there, but they are both really cool.'

'Okay, yeah. I'd really like that Sarah. I just want to come down off this now. I don't like it. Just let me say goodbye to Simon.' But when I look out into the back garden and see Simon and April huddled into a corner using a coin to do little hits of cocaine? I decide to just leave him to it. He doesn't look like he is going to miss me anyway.

Sarah was just incredible to me from the moment we left Sandra's house. I was having these waves of, well, I don't know what they were exactly. I just had these sporadic waves flow through me, and with each one I became more and more scared. I had completely lost control of my senses. And at the exact same time? I couldn't stop bloody talking! I never talk this much. What an absolute dickhead I am. I mean, what must Sarah think of me? Quite a lot as it turns out.

'Look, I'm going to tell my brother what's going on. Don't worry, he's cool. He just might know what to do with you now as you allow that crap to take its course.' And as soon as we arrived at her house, that is just what she did.

'Jaysus Jimmy. You are the last person I ever thought would do this,' says Sarah's brother, John. 'Don't worry pal – I've been exactly where you are once. We'll get ya through this. Many moons ago, I did the same as you Jimmy. I gave coke a try, and I instantly hated it. And thank god I did too. I've lost some amount of friends to that shite man. Between people not wanting to hang around with me for being a dry-shite, to people getting locked up – or worse! Shootings are *way* too common these days man, and most of those shootings are over that poxy little bag you now have in your pocket. Here, give it here.'

John holds out his had as I place what is left of my bag of coke into his palm. 'Come with me Jimmy, I want you to see this.' John leads me into a downstairs toilet, lifts up the toilet lid, and empties the bag of coke inside. He then flushes the toilet as he turns to me and says, 'See this shite Jimmy? It's just not worth it man – trust me.'

'I do trust you John,' I think, *'and I couldn't agree with you more.'*

'Right. Sarah? You're gonna have to keep an eye on him. He's not going to want to sleep, and he *may* want to talk about utter crap for most of the night. Just be there for him as best you can. You can crash here on the sofa tonight Jimmy, okay? And don't worry. It'll be over soon.'

A week has passed since that horrible night. Simon has been really off with me. I foolishly told him I flushed the coke (or at least John did), as it just wasn't for me.

'Why didn't ya fuckin' keep it, ya sap? You could have given it to me ya gobshite.' Simon has never spoken to me like this, and as much as I love the guy, I'm not having this.

'Screw you ya sap,' I reply, 'if you wanna walk around thinking the only way you can get a girl, or have a laugh, is by banging that shite up your nose? Well, you go ahead and do that. But don't you *dare* stand there and call me names just because I don't like it. I thought we were mates man?'

As annoyed as I am, I'm sure Simon could hear the sadness in my voice. But he didn't care.

'I don't want some pansy as a friend ya sap. You're lucky I'm not smashing your face in over that bag. It cost me €50 like.'

I see red. I feel like I want to rip Simon's head off, but instead I reach into my wallet and pull out a €50 note I earned from working in our local supermarket at the weekends. 'Here,' I say as I throw the note at him, 'here's your bleedin' money. So €50 is all our friendship is worth to you? Then here, take it!'

I am fighting back the tears when Simon hits me with, 'Us? Mates? Nah man! I hang around with the lads from the shops now yeah? And not one of them is a lightweight like you.'

I snap. I grab Simon, a lad who was once my best friend, by the scruff and pin him to the wall. 'Forget you, ya sap,' I say, 'and don't you ever call me a lightweight again. Besides, I'd rather be a lightweight than a jumped-up little coke-head like you. Have a good life, ya sap.' I let Simon go, turn around and walk away. And I never look back.

Almost two years have passed now since all that drama, and life has been pretty good to me. I did well in my Leaving Cert, and I got accepted into the local IT in order to do a Bachelors of Arts in Creative Digital Media. And guess who has a girlfriend now? Myself and Sarah just became closer and closer after that horrible night. I thought I'd messed up everything by doing coke and trying to be a 'mad yoke'. Thankfully, Sarah could see I was just being a dope. As for Simon? Sadly, I'm not too sure how he is. He began hanging around with the lads at the shops. I remember hearing his voice one day, and it had completely changed – like he was putting on a 'hard man's voice' to impress the gobshites around him. Himself and April had a baby boy too, although I think it's April's folks who are raising the child. Such a waste.

I am sitting on a bench facing the local cinema. I am patiently waiting for Sarah to meet me. She is coming straight from her shift in Penny's, and we are going to go watch a movie together. I got to pick the last time, so no doubt tonight will be that feckin' soppy movie everyone is harping on about. Still, I don't mind ... I'll be with Sarah.

It's not much longer until I catch sight of Sarah walking towards me. As she nears me, I can see she is almost bursting to tell me something. 'Hey,' she starts as she lightly kisses my cheek, 'look at this. But before you do? I must warn you. It might upset you.'

Sarah hands me her phone, and I see she has a news app opened. The headline read: *Twenty Year Old Male Sentenced to Five Years for Over €30,000 Worth of Cocaine.*

And as I navigate through the story, I stop dead. I finally look at Sarah but all she can say is, 'So sad.' The line that stopped me? *'Simon O'Rourke (20) from Finglas, Dublin, was sentenced to five years by Judge Nolan after being caught in possession of over €30,000 worth of cocaine...'*

My heart sunk. God Simon, what have you done? And even after all the crap that had come between us, my heart went out to him. For feck sake, Simon. Such a waste.

Discuss

♦ Is Simon a really bad guy, or just someone with really bad judgement?

♦ Is Sarah a 'wet-blanket,' or someone who really cares?

♦ Was Jimmy right to try cocaine because Simon made him feel it was a natural thing to do, even though Jimmy had doubts?

These are just some of the questions I came up with as I wrote this chapter for you. I'm sure you have many more, so please don't be afraid to ask them. Feel free to write down your thoughts on this chapter in the Personal Reflections section at the back of this book.

I am aware this chapter is rather hard-hitting, but drugs are literally destroying people's lives. And, unfortunately, and embarrassingly, I am telling you this from experience. I have taken cocaine. I am just so very, very lucky that cocaine didn't take me. My main poison was alcohol, but I got involved in this shitty world of drugs through my actions of being a drugs mule – and look what happened to me. Let me tell something for nothing, prison is hell on earth. You don't ever want to go there. And sadly, if you get involved in this life of drugs, the chances are you will see the inside of a prison cell. And that's if you are lucky. Why? Because you also could be killed.

I don't apologise for being blunt here because I am genuinely alarmed at the number of teens and young adults getting caught up in all of this. Look at the ages of some of those who have been gunned down lately. Some are in their early twenties, and many of their mates will never see their thirtieth birthday. Some have left children behind who now have no father. It's just not worth it.

So please – live your life drug-free. And if you are troubled or disturbed by any aspect of this chapter, please seek help. The sooner you do, the better you will feel. There are numbers you can ring at the back of this book.

6.

'I Will Always Miss You ...' – Josh's Story

Hey guys. It's Josh here again ... I told you I'd be back.
For me, this chapter is going to be difficult. If you remember, I mentioned earlier that I lost my dad in a road accident almost six years ago. And here's the thing – I still miss him as much today as I did when the news of this terrible accident was given to me. But today, I handle my grief in a different manner, one which is more beneficial to me. Sounds kinda selfish right? And I suppose it is, but when it comes to you and your mental health, I believe that you must put yourself first. If you're not okay with yourself, how can you expect others to be okay with you? This goes for all aspects of your life, but for now I would like to have a chat about grief. I will be completely honest, and share with you the emotions I went through, and in many ways am still going through, after my dad passed away.

Death is so final, and an unexpected death can really mess with your head. And sadly, most of you guys that are reading this have experienced the loss of someone in your life, be it an older relative who became ill and passed away, or a situation like mine and my dad's, where it was so sudden and unexpected. I hope the advice and help I received from others will help you, even in a small way, as you try to come to terms with loss.

So, I'm currently going through sixth year in school – my final year. Those of you who are also going through sixth year will know that it comes with its own stresses and worries. But what if you are trying to deal with grief at the same time? It adds a layer of sadness and loss on top of everything else.

I had actually just finished my Junior Cert when my dad passed away. I was numb. He was my hero. In the beginning I refused to believe he was gone. I won't go into any detail about the evening he died. It was a freak car accident, but that doesn't make it any easier. I'm pretty sure I cried so much when I heard that my body ran out of tears. Mam was distraught. That's the thing about death isn't it? It affects so many people, and it hardly ever affects two people in the exact same way. Maybe you can relate to this statement: *You almost feel guilty for grieving because someone else is upset too.* This is how I felt every time I saw my mam. She had just lost her husband – her best friend. So I felt guilty expressing my grief when I was around her. That was probably the biggest mistake I made. It is so important to express grief. But seeing my mam sitting alone in the kitchen with a photo of herself and my dad happy together, sobbing uncontrollably, actually made me feel guilty for missing my dad so much.

Everyone deals with grief in their own way. Some would have you believe that they are completely fine, some cry uncontrollably, some remain quiet and reserved, whereas some find comfort in remembering the happy times spent together. There is no right or wrong way to deal with death and loss. There is no guide book or instruction manual. There is only what's inside of you, so don't fight the feelings you experience. Share them, because the absolute worse thing you can do is bottle things up – as I found out the hard way.

My family crumbled after dad died. Although my two brothers were younger, they could still sense the grief as it hung in the air. Mam was surrounded by family and friends. Me? I was feeling crap, but I foolishly got it into my head that I could deal with it. *'Right! You are the eldest, so everyone needs you to be strong. No time for tears now.'* But who was I kidding? I was distraught. And yet, I still somehow managed to shove my grief further and deeper down inside of me, until I finally snapped. I found myself shouting at my beautiful mam one day and realised I needed help – fast!

I literally roared at her in the kitchen one morning. I yelled at her that she *'didn't care how I felt – she didn't understand what I was going through.'* Did she get angry with me? Did she yell back and throw me out of the kitchen? No, she didn't, even if I deserved it. Instead, she pulled out a chair from our kitchen table and just flopped down onto it. Her head fell into her hands and she just cried and cried. And then? She turned to me and said, 'I'm sorry if I've let you down, Josh. I'm trying son, I really am.'

I felt like shit, but hearing those words from my mam made the dam burst. Soon, I am sitting next to her sobbing as she cradles my head to her chest. 'Oh Josh. I'm so worried about you,' says my mam, 'you don't talk to us about how you feel.'

'I know mam. I just don't want to upset you,' I reply through tears.

'But, *you* are upset Josh, and that needs to be dealt with too.' As always, mam was right. I had a penny-drop moment in the kitchen that day. I knew I needed to talk, but found it hard to talk to my family. So I sought out the help of a counsellor, and it was the best decision I have ever made. We teens put some silly notions into our own minds sometimes, right? Like, if you ask for help you are weak, or if you cry you are a sap. Ridiculous. Seeking help when you are struggling is a sign of strength.

The chats between myself and my counsellor are private, as will your chats be too, so I won't go into too much detail here. What I can say is that a combination of counselling and talking to both my friends and family about how I feel is the reason I am in the positive headspace I am today. Will I ever 'get over' my dad's death? I doubt it very much. Do I deal with his loss better today? I do, one hundred per cent.

I want to share with you something I heard during one my sessions with my counsellor – something that really helped me.

'Josh, I want you to picture a spider's web. Just a regular little house spider's web, like the ones we see all the time. If we took a photo of this web and zoomed in, we would see that this web is actually quite beautiful. It is made up of tiny silk strings, is very complex and has a wonderful, intricate design. It is amazing to think that such a little creature can create something so beautiful and so complex.

Now, let's just say we became really cruel all of a sudden. Imagine if we got a pen and we plucked just one of these tiny silk strings … what would happen? That's right, the beautiful web would collapse. By simply pulling at one string, we destroy all this little spider's hard work.

But here's the thing ... If we go back to that web some days later, we will see that the spider has built a whole new web ... just as beautiful, just as intricate, just as complex, and yet, completely new and different.

When your dad died, one of your silk strings from your own web was plucked, Josh. And when it was plucked, your entire web collapsed. But you too have strength and skills like that little spider, and in time, you will begin to rebuild your web. It won't be the same, but it will be just as beautiful, just as intricate, and just as complex. And never be afraid to ask for help as you rebuild.'

I really hope that helps anyone out there dealing with grief.

Finally, I just want to remind you of two really important statements: 'It's okay not to be okay,' and, 'It's so important to talk.' These words of wisdom continue to help me today, and they can help you too.

Discuss

♦ Was Josh right to think he couldn't share his grief with his mam?

♦ Is Josh strong or weak for asking for help?

These are just some of the questions I came up with as I wrote this chapter for you. I'm sure you have many more, so please don't be afraid to ask them. Feel free to write down your thoughts on this chapter in the Personal Reflections section at the back of this book.

This was a hard chapter to write, and I'm sure a hard one for you to read. But sadly, death and loss play a huge part *in all our lives, so I feel it is vital to seek help and support in order to cope. Remember, no two people grieve the same. What works for me may not work for you. But I think we can all agree that talking and seeking help are a good way to start the healing process.*

The character of Josh is based on an amazing young man I met in the Holy Family School in Rathcoole. He was there the day I met 'K,' and every time I looked around, this young man was doing all he could to help those who were upset around him. But when I had a moment on my own with him, I learned that he had just recently lost his dad. I couldn't believe how mature he was. He informed me that he knew he needed help, so he went and got it. And now that he is in a better place, he wants to help as many as he can. He is sixteen years of age folks!

And the spider web story? I sadly lost my baby daughter when I was only seventeen, and to this day I'm still not 'over it'. But I try to deal with it in a positive way. That spider web analogy helped me so much.

7.

'No Means No'
– Maeve's Story

The last day of school is *finally* upon us, although I shouldn't really complain. This last school year has been fantastic. Almost all of the girls in my class decided to do fourth year, or 'Transition Year' as it is known. After completing the Junior Cert, and doing a lot better than I had anticipated, it was nice to enter a school year where the stress levels decreased somewhat.

'Maeve!' I hear my name being shouted from behind me as I make my way towards the massive iron gates of my school. I'd know that voice anywhere – Gill, my best friend, a friend so good that I believe everyone should have a Gill in their lives. She is shorter than I am, although most people are as I am almost six feet! Gill has flowing red hair, and her face is covered with the cutest freckles you have ever seen.

'Hi Gill,' I start, 'all set for our last day?' I ask Gill this while displaying the biggest smile I can muster.

'Maeve, it's like my whole year has been building up to this moment. No more getting up early on the weekdays, no more Miss Cunningham and her constant droning about the importance of becoming a vegan.' This last assessment Gill has made of Miss Cunningham, our 'social studies' teacher, unites us both in laughter.

'I know Gill,' I say, 'but I think it's kinda nice how much Miss Cunningham cares. Anyway, you look great Gill – although you always do.'

'Awwee, thanks Maeve,' replies Gill in a shy manner, followed by, 'and this coming from the six foot blonde super model.'

Now it's my turn to become shy. I may get a lot of attention from boys my age, but I promise you I don't look for it. I'm not really that confident. But my mam helps me out so much with this aspect of my life.

'Maeve, you are beautiful, inside and out. And no, this is not just your mam saying that ... it's just simply the truth.'

My mam is great looking as well. In her younger years she did some modelling. I love looking at the photos from some of her shoots. I sometimes look at them in disbelief. Like, *this is my mam!* Sadly, my mother's beauty wasn't enough for my dad. They split up about two years ago, and almost instantly dad found someone else. Is she as beautiful as my mam? God no! Did I give dad's new girlfriend a hard time when I first met her? Embarrassingly, yes. And believe it or not, it was my mam who reprimanded me.

'Dad is entitled to be happy, Maeve. I know you are worried about me, but when have I ever given you, or anyone for that matter, reason to be concerned?' My mam was right. She is the strongest woman I know. She is always reminding me how important it is to speak your mind. She gives wise, sometimes funny advice about boys too. Boys my age can be sooo immature sometimes. Yep, my mam is great, and yet I am still keeping a massive secret from her. Why? Maybe because I am confused myself? Maybe because I'm not sure how she will take it? Maybe…

Myself and Gill soon find ourselves huddled in a circle with our friends, and all we can talk about is Cameron's house party later. 'I can't wait girls,' starts Gill, 'I'm actually gonna ask Gavin if he wants to be my boyfriend! Like, we've been shifting for the past *ages*…'

'Uggh,' we gasp collectively, which makes Gill laugh.

'Why are *you* asking *him* Gill? Let him ask you!' This question/statement is made by Mary. Mary is a really cool girl with mousy-brown hair cut into a bob, and a smile that can light up an entire room.

'It's 2019,' I respond, 'why can't us women take the lead, eh? My mam is always saying I should be the strongest woman I can be. She actually makes perfect sense.' The girls all nod in agreement.

'Besides,' starts Gill, 'if I don't ask him, it will *never* happen. You know what boys are like.' This brings a collective 'amen' from the girls.

'*Yeah,*' I think to myself, '*boys are just silly…*'

The last hours of school fly by and soon we are all saying our goodbyes at the school gates. Arrangements are made to meet up in Gill's this evening, and then we can all go as a group to Cameron's. Am I as thrilled as the other girls for tonight's get-together? Sadly not. This may sound like I'm being vain, but I promise you, nothing could be further from the truth. It's just that I get a lot of attention from boys sometimes. My mam is great about this: '*You are a lovely girl, so drink in the compliments. But if a boy is annoying you, just calmly and nicely explain you're not interested.*

And if he keeps it up? Then explain, in no uncertain terms, that No means No!' My mam always gives the best advice.

After spending what seemed like a lifetime choosing something to wear, I settle on a floral maxi dress and some sandals. I have decided to wear my hair up, and when Gill answers her front door she gasps, 'Oh, you are sooo stunning, ya bitch!' I can feel my face turn a bright shade of red.

'Shut up you ya big eejit,' I reply, 'besides, just look at *you*.' She had on a cool Guns 'N' Roses T-Shirt, combined with some light denim jeans and some white runners. Simple right? But Gill can make simple look fabulous.

We all arrive at Cameron's and it is immediately clear that poor ol' Cameron invited way too many people. Every now and then, he can be heard shouting, 'Jaysis, watch my mam's feckin' vase, will ya?' or, 'There is *another* toilet upstairs, so can you *please* not pee out in my back garden?' Poor ol' Cameron.

The party is in full swing. Myself and all the girls are dancing to a Taylor Swift song – well, all the girls accept Gill. 'Where is ... ahhh, here she comes,' I say. We all stop dancing as Gill approaches arm in arm with Gavin, both of them with huge smiles across their faces.

'He said "yes", naturally,' laughs Gill. Gavin looks morto having to stand there in front of us all, but he seems happy as well.

'Here, Maeve?' says Gavin, a tall skinny lad with black hair, 'Fran is looking for you everywhere. He's a bit locked, so you have been warned.'

'*Great,*' I think to myself. Don't get me wrong, I like Fran, as a friend. I'm just not in the mood of him asking me cringy things like, 'Was your dad a thief? Because he robbed the stars and put them in your eyes.' God! Still, he is pretty harmless I suppose.

Suddenly, I hear a shout. 'Maeve!' It's Fran. 'Are your feet hurting you? Because you've been running through my mind all night.'

God!! 'Heya Fran, you look, eh, well, you look drunk actually,' I say.

'Ah, I'm grand,' replies Fran, 'can I talk to you for a second?'

'Sure,' I say. We head out into Cameron's huge back garden. There are some partygoers having a breather out here, while others have come out for a snog away from prying eyes. Fran talks away as he leads me towards a wooden bench at the bottom of the garden. I suppose Fran is a good-looking guy. Short, strawberry-blonde hair and kinda cute dimples when he smiles ... if that's what you're into.

We've literally only put our bums on the bench when Fran says, 'I'm *mad* into you Maeve. Like, I'm thinkin' about you all the time, ya know?' He kinda slurs this at me. Not the most attractive look I can tell you.

'I am very flattered Fran,' I reply, 'but I am really happy with our friendship so I don't want to ruin that.'

I am hoping this will soften the blow for Fran, but I find I'm a little shocked when he says, 'Ah, but you know you feel the same. I can tell by how ya talk to me an' all.'

This annoys me a little, but I manage to keep my composure and say, 'Look Fran. Don't act the maggot here okay? I am trying to be nice...'

Fran interrupts by saying, 'Can I kiss you?'

'*No!*' I reply, in fact, I almost shout this at him.

'Ah, come on Maeve,' Fran says. But then? Then he did something that made me feel so uncomfortable. He took a firm hold of my left arm, just below my elbow, and began pulling me towards him. I was shocked at first. Although Fran can be ultra-annoying sometimes, I have never seen him act this way. My mam's words come flooding into my brain: '*No Means No!*'

I pull my arm back with force, and once it's free, I use it to grab Fran by the scruff of his white shirt. 'What the *hell* do you think you're doing? Did you not hear me? I said *no*, and *no means no Fran*!' I am yelling at him now. I'm not sure if it is fear, adrenaline, or anger that is coursing through me, but once Fran sees how upset I am, he is shocked – so shocked in fact, that he almost sobers up.

'What am I doing? I'm a fucking scumbag Maeve. I am so, so sorry.' Fran begins sobbing as these words leave his mouth.

'Fran, what the hell', I say. 'This isn't you. But I am not going to allow you to blame the drink on this. How dare you not respect my wishes? How *dare* you!'

'Ah Maeve. I know, I know. He is crying uncontrollably now. 'Should I go home?' Fran looks at me with sadness and embarrassment etched all over his face.

'Yes, I think that would be a good idea Fran.' I feel a little guilty saying this, but I'm hoping my sternness will be a constant reminder to Fran that he needs to learn about 'consent'. I tell him he should leave and that I want to see him tomorrow when he is sober so we can talk through what just happened.

'Please don't say anything, okay?' pleads Fran.

'Just get yourself home and we'll talk tomorrow.' Part of me is dying inside as I talk to Fran in this manner. But he has got to learn.

The next morning I wake up feeling like crap. Why in god's name did Fran have to do that? I was so upset when Fran left last night that I faked a headache and left early myself. But this morning, I am determined that I want to have this out with Fran. I pick up my phone and proceed to ring him.

'Ehhh, hello?' comes the half-asleep greeting from Fran.

'It's me, Maeve. I'll see you in Starbucks in the village in a half hour, okay?'

'Yeah, yeah, sure, okay. Thanks Maeve. Are you okay?' asks Fran.

'Of course I'm not, you gobshite,' I reply.

Thirty-six minutes later in sulks Fran, and as he makes his way towards my table, he has already begun apologising. 'Maeve ... I just want to to know how truly sorry I am.'

'Sit down Fran, and listen very carefully,' I say, as I note the anger in my own voice. 'You shocked me last night Fran,' I say, 'of all the boys, I *never* thought you would do something like that. I said "no" Fran, and I bloody well meant it!' I find I am becoming more angry, so I decide to allow him to grovel.

'I swear Maeve, I completely "get" consent. I know how important it is today. I told my dad what I did and he was really angry. He kept saying, "how could you be so stupid" over and over, and as he did, the gravity of what I had done hit me.'

Fran is clearly upset now. But I don't offer any condolence.

He continues, 'I told my dad I was meeting you, and he told me to tell you the truth about why I might have done something so dumb. I thought about it, and could only come up with, *"I didn't think you'd mind"*. What an arsehole I am, Maeve. I'm so sorry.'

Fran then continues, 'And do you know what is worse? I did that Consent Class in school a few weeks back. I learned so much about consent that day. Like, the importance of requiring consent in *all aspects* of your life. For example, where I work at the weekends, I was allowing my supervisor to dump a lot of his work on top of mine. I learned that he should ask for my consent before doing so, and not just assume I won't mind. And, believe it or not, we spoke at length about consent when it comes to sex and all that. And yet, I *still* did that last night. Obviously I'd had a few drinks, but I know that is no excuse. I messed up big-time and I am disgusted with myself. And I also know I have now lost a good friend.'

I sit back in my chair, and I feel a wave of relief flow through me. I was convinced I was going to have to educate Fran on the many different avenues of consent, but listening to him has shown me he is well clued in. Sadly, though, that kinda makes last night more difficult to deal with.

'I can see how sorry you are Fran, and I appreciate your honesty, but you need to think long and hard about what you did. Doing something like that could get you into serious trouble, Fran, and you could get a bad reputation that will stick with you for life.'

'Thanks, Maeve, and I am so grateful that you met me this morning. Ah shit ... here comes Gill. Will I just go? She probably hates my guts!'

I turn to see Gill's beaming smile as she walks towards us. I spin around in my chair, look at Fran and say, 'I didn't tell anyone Fran. I wanted to give you a chance this morning.'

Fran looks relieved as I turn to Gill and say, 'Hey girl, what's new?'

'Feck all,' starts Gill, 'I just saw you two lovebirds all snuggled up, so I wanted to get all the gossip. So, come on, are you both "official" now?'

I'm pretty both our faces turned the same shade of crimson as Fran stutters, 'Eh, ah, n-no, we're just friends.'

'And we're barely even that sometimes,' I add with a laugh.

'Aw, but you're both sooo cute together,' says Gill, 'besides, you never really settle with any of the lads, Maeve. What's up with that?'

I want the ground to swallow me whole. I am morto!

Gill doesn't see this and continues, 'Like, I can't remember the last boy you snogged, not that snogging is the *be all and end all*, but like, I honestly can't remember the last...'

'*I like girls okay?!?*' I almost shout this. Shit! What the hell just happened? Why have I just blurted this out *now*? I have been dealing with these feelings about my sexuality completely on my own for so long ... and now? Now Gill *and bloody Fran* know!

Well? It's out there now. Shit! But I suppose, in for a penny, in for a pound, so somehow I continue, 'I'm not sure when I realised. For so long I thought it was just a phase (I can feel the tears coming). I kinda ignored it and thought I was being silly. But I know it to be true. I like girls Gill ... I'm gay. I'm gay and my own mother doesn't even know. Why the hell can't I tell her Gill? Why am I so afraid to tell *anyone*?'

Gill almost leaps across the table and embraces me in a bear hug, while poor Fran is sitting there looking like a rabbit caught in the headlights. 'I am so super-proud of you,' says Gill, 'sooo proud. Who cares if you are attracted to the same sex these days? Love is love, and everyone deserves to be loved.'

I'm roaring crying now. I was afraid of uttering those words for so long. I feared the mocking, bullying, abuse. But I never pictured this. Gill being so supportive, and Fran looking so confused, like he is trying to learn Chinese!

'And as for your mam?' says Gill, 'we'll both go to her, *right now*, and we will tell her together. She'll be fine. Me? I'm just so excited now that I get to go to the gay bars with you when we're older. My cousin Mark? He's gay and always talking about this great club in town. He says they are the best nights ever. I'm so excited.'

Fran, who was still smarting from our converstation, tries to bring some humour to the situation. 'Like, I'm happy for ya, Maeve,' he says, 'but I suppose this means I've *no feckin' chance* with you now!' Fran erupts into laughter at his own joke but it did the job. I find myself smiling.

Wow. So, I eventually came out, in a Starbucks, *after* dressing down a friend over consent. My mam is right – I don't do thinks by half.

It's been almost two years since that fateful day. Fran found love with a really nice girl named Lisa and Gill has become an even closer friend. I even told her I had a tiny crush on her, which she took really well. In fact, she likes to mock me about it every now and then.

She came with me that morning to tell my mam, and I have no idea what I was so worried about. My mam looked at me when I told her and she asked, 'Do you feel happy now that we all know? Do you feel like you?'

Of course I answered 'yes,' and when I did, my mother's smile just grew and grew. And today, somehow, she is even more supportive than ever.

I met someone too – Jenny. She is amazing. And on the night we first kissed? We both knew we had each other's consent – and it was the greatest kiss of my life.

Discuss

♦ Is it ever okay to blame being drunk on your bad actions, like how drunk Fran was when he upset Mave?

♦ Did Maeve handle the whole situation of consent well?

♦ Do you fully understand consent yourself?

♦ Was Maeve right to fear coming out?

♦ Is Gill a good friend?

These are just some of the questions I came up with as I wrote this chapter for you. I'm sure you have many more, so please don't be afraid to ask them. Feel free to write down your thoughts on this chapter in the Personal Reflections section at the back of this book.

Consent – *a word that holds so much power today. I'm sure you are well aware about what consent means, but on the other hand I feel the lines of consent have become blurred. Again, I feel it is vital for us all to have a conversation about this, and I hope that is what you will do with your family and friends. In the case of Maeve, we can be thankful that nothing more serious happened between herself and Fran. But what did happen in the story above was unacceptable and highlights the need to be clear about consent. So please,* *know your worth and your boundaries in every aspect of your life. And be mindful of other people too when it comes to consent. Don't ever be afraid to spark a conversation about it.*

Coming Out – *Thankfully, we have become a more welcoming and understanding planet. Who cares who you love? Love is love, and we are all entitled to experience it in every way possible. Can you relate to Maeve in this story? If so, my advice is to not do other people's thinking for them. Don't assume people are going to judge or hate or mock you. Just stand tall and be proud of who you are. If you're struggling with your sexuality, please talk to someone you trust, or maybe ring one of the numbers provided at the back of this book.*

And as this chapter ends, please allow the two phrases below to seep into your soul:

No Means No.

Love is Love.

8.

'The Bully and the Bullied' – Justin and David's Story

'Justin'

Wednesday: 8.32 am

I just about finish chapter thirty-four in volume two of *Percy Jackson and the Olympians,* when I hear my dad calling my name from the bottom of our staircase. 'Justin. Let's go buddy.'

'Coming dad,' comes my reply. God. I really wish I could bring this book into school with me today. It has me gripped. I love books like this – fantasy books. Books where the characters are usually vampires or wizards, or in the case of the book I am currently reading, gods – The Olympians and The Titans. I swear, it's sooo good! But I wouldn't dare bring it into school with me. I'd be crucified, mocked, made to feel like utter crap, this all coming from one lad and his band of merry fools. David, or 'D-man' as his cohorts refer to him, took an instant dislike to me on the very first day of school last year. I was already feeling quite nervous, so when David decided to push me over in front of everyone, for no reason that I can think of, I knew the year ahead was going to be a bumpy one. Like, I've never got why he pushed me that morning. He mentioned something about my glasses I think...

Since fifth class, I've had a massive complex. I badly needed glasses, and when I got them, I kinda became the butt of my fellow classmates' jokes. It really hurt. It stripped me of my confidence and made me feel that, in some way, I almost deserve to be mocked. Sometimes I also feel like I make myself into an easy target. For example, I don't follow a football team. I am *brutal* at most sports actually, except running. But I'm usually the last one picked in P.E. Which is fine by me actually. I'd rather I wasn't picked at all to be fair. Football, basketball ... they're just not my thing. Reading? Allowing your mind to wander as the author takes you on a journey? Now, *that's* my thing. But why does my 'thing' make me a target for bullies?

'Justin, come on man. I'll be late for work.' My dad is great. He makes me feel like I can accomplish anything. I sometimes wish I could share his love for his beloved Manchester City, but in no way does he make me feel like a failure or a 'let-down' because I don't. And what's even better is how my dad goes above and beyond to learn as much as he can about *my* interests. I sometimes see smoke coming out of his ears when I talk about a 'Death Crawler, stalking the enchanted forest,' but he gives it a go, and he does this for me. Yet, I am too embarrassed to tell my dad about David. Why? I'm not sure. This whole situation has just made me feel so weak and pathetic. No wonder I love to get lost in a world of fantasy.

Wednesday: 9.02 am

I say my goodbyes to dad, and allow his final words to linger, *'There is nothing you can't do buddy. Once you believe in youresel? Jobs a good-un.'* I have no idea what 'jobs a good-un' means, but I assume it's something like, 'everything will work out fine.'

I see my best friend, Brandon, heading towards me. We both kinda look the same (short, tubby, with brown hair), which is weird, but we both also share the same interests ... which is great. 'Hey Justin,' says Brandon. 'So, I finished volume two last night. Ahh man, you won't *believe* what Tho...'

'Eh? Shut up Brandon,' I interject, 'I'm only about half-way through. *No spoilers.*'

Brandon laughs as he says, 'I was only joking. I am, and shall remain, fully compliant on the ethics of spoilers. In other words? My lips are sealed man.'

'Ah look, it's Dork and Dorky, the two Dorks!'

Great – It's David! David is a skinny lad with a shock of jet-black hair.

'What's new girls? Read any new witch books or whatever the hell they are? Bleedin' weirdos. Am I right boys?' David has turned to his posse, and like the faithful little fools they are, they all kinda grunt and nod in agreement.

I look around and catch the eye of some of my fellow students, but most of them look away as soon as I meet their gaze. I suppose David's attack on myself and Brandon has nothing got to do with them and they don't want to get involved. Maybe they fear him too, or maybe they just don't care. I really wish I could stand up for myself. I really, *really* wish David would leave me alone.

But as I turn and walk away, David begins laughing and shouting, 'Wide-load coming through ... clear a space lads, will ya?'

I want to dissolve ... disappear. Why me?

Wednesday: 12.54 pm

'... and I expect those assignments on my desk first thing lads, okay?' Mr. Clarke, our geography teacher, has just handed out the biggest pile of homework my young eyes have ever seen. Still, I relish hard work, and I have a thirst for knowledge. I want to make something of my life, just like my dad did.

'Now, remember boys, all classes are cancelled after lunch, as we welcome Aunua Academy and their speakers into our school. And I said "welcome" David!' Mr. Clarke fixes David with a glare, which clearly makes David feel uncomfortable. I love it! 'These folks today are coming in as part of our mental health week lads, so I highly recommend you open your minds to what they have to say.'

As if on cue, the school's bell rings out from the intercom above the classroom door. Brandon has a hospital appointment later today, so unfortunately he will miss the speakers. I make my way out of the classroom and head into the toilet. What I didn't notice was David coming in behind me. Suddenly, I am shoved face first to the ground. I feel a tooth bite down on my bottom lip, and soon I can taste blood as it seeps from the wound. All I can hear is laughter coming from David and Harry, David's most loyal sidekick. Harry looks like feckin' 'Hagrid' from *Harry Potter*. But I won't be telling him *that* any time soon.

'Get up nerd,' begins David, 'come on ... *up*. You think you're so special cuz you always do well in a test? You think you're so much better than I am because you like to read? I'm sick of you, ya little dork!'

From somewhere, I don't know where, I summon the strength to reply. 'What in the hell have I *ever* done to you David? You just don't like...'

Smack!

Wednesday: 1.18 pm

My tears have stopped, thankfully. I catch sight of myself in the toilet's filthy mirror. I can't believe he hit me. He just hit me, and walked out. Even Harry looked shocked. He just hit me. I can't believe it. I can't take this anymore. I just can't do this anymore. I'm going to have to tell a teacher on him ... shit! That will just bring more carnage my way. I need help. I need my dad.

I make up my mind to tell my dad everything once I'm home. I just don't want him becoming Bruce Lee and going all 'ninja' on David or his family. But I need help. I can't take this anymore.

My cheek is really hurting. It felt like he kinda slapped me across the face. Thankfully, my glasses are still intact. I use countless tissues to clean up my face, and soon I look – well, I look like shit. But sure, nobody but Brandon notices me in here, so no one will be able to tell.

Wednesday: 3.12 pm

Wow. Talk about being on a rollercoster of emotions. I've gone from being slapped across the face by David and feeling like dirt to feeling like the most special, most capable human alive! Jesus. These Aunua Academy guys are good. We have already listened to their founder as she spoke so openly and lovingly about us teens. We have had a life-coach instilling in us some great techniques to help handle the daily grind of teen life, a motivational speaker who is non-verbal, and yet gave the most moving and inspiring talk ever through a computer, and now I am sitting listening to a former prisoner – and he has us gripped. He is crazy. He has let foul language slip out, he even cried at one stage, which in turn made some of the lads, including myself, cry too. But now? Right now, he's talking about bullying, and he's getting very angry about it. Yes! I look over at David. He too is transfixed on this man as he rants about the damage a bully can do. For the first time, it is I who feels like the 'big man', while I kinda hope David feels really small.

The speaker then lowers his voice. His tone changes. He looks at every students' face as he says, 'I can completely understand a young person wanting to fight a bully back. I can completely understand if your mam or dad actually encouraged you to do it. But today, I want to give you another avenue to maybe think about, should you ever find yourself being bullied. My advice? Don't fight back. Instead, make yourself strong. And no, I don't mean head down to the bleedin' gym and start pumping iron. I'm talking about having the strongest mind you can. The brain, our mind, these are muscles that need working out too. So, think of it like this:

'Usually, a bully will pick on you because you are "different". But I ask you? Different in whose eyes? In his or hers? So what? If you are lucky enough to be different from the norm, then why would you want to change? But it still hurts right? I get that. So, if we become ultra-strong in our minds ... if we love the stuffing out of who we are, what we do, and how we live our life? And if we are truly happy with the person we are, then the negative opinions of others will mean nothing to us. Someone else's opinion of you is actually none of your business, so let them have it. Is their opinion about you true? Absolutely not. So fuck them and let them have their stupid opinion. Because once you truly love and believe in yourself? Then no hurtful or negative opinions from morons can hurt you.'

I am glued to this speaker's every word, when suddenly I feel my left arm reaching high above my head. What the hell am I doing?

'Yes,' says the speaker, 'young man in the middle there. Have you a question buddy?'

Every student, including David, has turned to look at me as I say, in a tone of utter defeat, 'What if they just keep hitting you?'

The speaker looks at me for what feels like a lifetime and then says, 'Don't ever let anyone get away with just hitting you. If you feel the need to hit back? Then hit back. Just be mindful that you are now engaged in a fight and if caught, you will *both* be punished. If fighting back just isn't an option, then go to your folks, or your closest family member or friend, or a teacher, and tell them everything. This isn't 'ratting'. You shouldn't have to put up with crap like this, so go to an adult you trust. They will know what to do. I hope that answers your question young man, and please feel free to chat to me later if you need to.'

I didn't need to. I needed to get home and see my dad.

The entire room was on its feet applauding this man after his talk. I am so grateful for our school for bringing Aunua Academy into us today. This is a day I will never forget.

As I walked home, I began practicing in my mind the words I was going to use to tell my dad about David. I find myself at the traffic lights facing the park, and when I look up to cross the street, I see David standing on the other side. I freeze in fear, but then strangely, David simply lowers his head, turns and walks away.

Wednesday: 7.43 pm

What a day. From being slagged and slapped to feeling like I can take on the world. My head is, quite literally, spinning. I have honestly taken on board all the information I have received from the speakers of Aunua with gusto. I have realised my own worth. I know how important I am. And I am proud as punch that I like books more than football!

I've called my dad into the sitting room for a chat. I'm ready for this. And he is going to be so proud of me. Why? Because from today, I am going to believe in *his* opinion of me, and *my* opinion of myself. I will *never again* believe the negative opinions of others towards me. *I Am Enough!*

'Everything okay Justin?' asks dad. I smile, and say the next words with so much conviction:

'I am okay dad. I had a problem I was keeping from you, and I want to tell you about it now. But I promise dad ... I'm okay.'

And for the first time in I don't know how long? I really was.

'David'

Wednesday: 8.32 am

'Look at the bleedin' state of ya, ya little gobshite. Get out of my sight an' feck off to school ya little toe-rag. And ha! School? Like you'll ever amount to anything ya little sap.'

'*Morning to you too da,*' I think to myself. How me ma puts up with him and his drinkin' is beyond me. Every bleedin' day that man finds time to tell me what a screw-up I am. Every day, including weekends, his drunken gob spits words of utter disgust at me. My personal favourite? *'You'll amount to nothin'.'* Can I be honest with you? It really, *really* hurts. I just can't tell anyone it does. No *way!*

I remember one day, bleedin' yonks ago, we were all down at the stadium for a fun-run. That little sap Justin was there with his 'perfect dad'. It made me want to vomit as I sat there listening to his auld fella: *'Go on son. You can do it son. We all believe in ya son!'* My da? He was locked, and when I tripped towards the end of the 100 metre sprint, I could actually hear him laughing at me. Shitehawk! And all the while, there's that sap Justin rubbing his perfect da into my face. Bleedin' dork so he is. Sure, he doesn't even like football! I mean, who doesn't like football? He'd rather read a book. *A bleedin' book!* Yeah, he thinks he's better than me. Ah, but c'mere and I tell ya. See the first day of school last year? I shoved him in front of the lads. Ha! Oh how we all laughed. Flyin' he went. And he didn't even fight back. Wimp. I knew right there and then that he would be easy pickings.

Bleedin' Justin, always thinking you're better than me.

Wednesday: 9.02 am

I meet the lads at the top of the school road, and we all head into school together. The lads are alright. They all think I'm mad, so they just kinda do what I say. Saps.

'Here D-man, look. It's yer man Brandon and *your mate* Justin,' says Harry, probably the only real friend I've got. He looks like yer man from the *Harry Potter* films, 'Hagger' or whatever ya call him!

'D-Man' is what the boys call me. I like it to be honest. 'C'mon let's head over and wreck their heads D-Man,' says Pauly, a stocky lad with fire-red hair.

I don't need to be asked twice. Besides, the lads expect nothing less from me. We make our way over and as soon as I am in ear shot of 'Perfect Justin', I shout, 'Ah look, it's Dork and Dorky, the two Dorks! What's new girls? Read any new witch books or whatever the hell they are? Bleedin' weirdos. Am I right boys?'

All the lads start falling around laughing. Poor auld Justin looks like he might cry like a little baba, so he turns to walk away. *'Not on my watch,'* I think, *'I'm not finished with you yet Perfect Justin.'* 'Wide-load coming through ... clear a space lads will ya?'

All the lads are in stitches again. Ha! It feels good to be bad sometimes, ya know?

Wednesday: 12.54 pm

'... and I expect those assignments on my desk first thing lads okay?' Auld fella Clarke, our geography teacher. I can't stand geography, and I can't stand him. Although, I get the impression that the feeling is mutual.

'Now, remember boys, all classes are canceled after lunch, as we welcome Aunua Academy and their speakers into our school. And I said "welcome" David!' The sap is staring straight at me. The neck of him, tryin' to make a fool out of me. Of course, no one noticed 'Perfect Justin' and 'Big-Boy Brandon' yapping away while Clarke continued to talk.

'These folks today are coming in as part of our mental health week lads, so I highly recommend you open your minds to what they have to say.' Just as he finishes his last words, the school's bell comes blaring out of the intercom. I'm *out* the door before the bell stops ringing. I wait for Harry, and as I do, I spot Justin heading into the toilet. Harry arrives and I say, 'Come on. I wanna teach someone a lesson once and for all.'

We sneak in behind Justin, and before he has a chance to turn around, I shove him! He goes face first, onto the floor. Ha! Myself and Harry fall about laughing. 'Perfect Justin' tries to get up, and I notice blood on his lip. Serves him right. 'Get up nerd,' I roar, 'come on ... *up*. You think you're so special cuz you always do well in a test? You think you're so much better than me because you like to read? I'm sick of you ya little dork!'

All of a sudden, Justin grows a spine. He gets off the ground, and if I'm honest, the look in his eyes is scaring me a little. 'What in the hell have I *ever* done to you David?' cries Justin, 'you just don't like...'

Smack!

Wednesday: 1.18 pm

'Ha! Did ya see his face Harry? He didn't see *that* comin' now did he? Little dork.' I say this to Harry as we both share a smoke in the lane across from the schools gates.

'Yeah D-man, he looked shocked alright. I kinda felt bad if I'm honest,' says Harry.

'Bad? Why? For what? Are you turning into a pansy on me or something Harry?' comes my reply.

'Eh, n-no,n-no man, like, I'm just sayin'...'

'Yeah, well don't "just say" anything Harry,' I interrupt. The truth is, Harry is only mirroring what I'm thinking myself. I too feel kinda bad for hitting him. Those words he was saying, just before I slapped him, '*What in the hell have*

I ever done to you David?' They are playing over and over in my mind. Truth is, Justin has actually never done anything to me ... ever. I am actually starting to feel guilty. Jaysis – what's come over me?

Wednesday: 3.12 pm

Ah man. What the hell is goin' on? These mad feckers from this Aunua Academy have kinda got into my head. There was this woman and she was telling us her story and how she created Aunua to help as many youths as she possibly can. Some 'life coach' or somethin' started giving us advice on how we speak to ourselves. And listening to her, I realised I speak to myself like shit. I mirror what my da says about me. I am allowing myself to believe that he's right – *'I'll never amount to anything.'* That life coach was amazing.

And then this lady spoke to us, through a computer as she is non-verbal, and she completely blew me away. I actually felt myself getting bleedin' emotional an' all, but I kept that in.

And now, there is some mad fecker, a former prisoner (I wonder does he know my da? He's been in and out of The Joy all his bleedin' life), and he's on a mad one. Roaring at us, even swearing sometimes! But now? Now I want the ground to swallow me. Now he's talking about bullying. Shit, he's even *crying* now in front of us. Shit – so am I. Pull yourself together D-Man, ya sap! The speaker then lowers his voice. His tone changes. He looks at every students' face as he begins to say, 'I can completely understand a young person wanting to fight a bully back. I can completely understand if your mam or dad actually encouraged you to do it. But today, I want to give you another avenue to maybe think about, should you ever find yourself being bullied.

My advice? Don't fight back. Instead, make yourself strong. And no, I don't mean head down to the bleedin' gym and start pumping iron. I'm talking about having the strongest mind you can. The brain, our mind, these are muscles that need working out too. So, think of it like this:

'Usually, a bully will pick on you because you are 'different.' But I ask you? Different in whose eyes? In his or her eyes? So what? If you are lucky enough to be different from the norm, then why would you want to change? But it still hurts right? I get that. So, if we become ultra strong in our minds, if we love the stuffing out of who we are, what we do, and how we live our life, then the negative opinions of others will mean nothing to us. Someone else's opinion of you is actually none of your business, so let them have it. Is their opinion about you true? Absolutely not. So fuck them and let them have their stupid opinion. Because once you truly love and believe in yourself? Then no hurtful or negative opinions from morons can hurt you.'

Ah man! I feel like shit, utter shit. I look to my right and catch sight of Harry's face and I can tell he feels exactly the same. What have we done? Not only has this speaker held a mirror in front of myself and Harry and made us see what horrible people we are for what we have done to Justin, he has also made me realise that I shouldn't have to listen to my da at home when he's calling me those names. I should believe in myself, not in his drunken bullshit. But, do I deserve a chance? After all I have done to Justin, do I actually deserve a chance? I turn to look over at Justin and see he has his hand up. Shit! He's gonna rat on me, although, let's face it, it's all I deserve. But Justin doesn't rat, instead he says, 'What if they just keep hitting you?' Jaysis man ... he sounds defeated. Ahh shit, what have I done. The speaker looks at Justin for what feels like a lifetime and then says, 'Don't ever let anyone away with just hitting you. If you feel the want to hit back? Then hit back. Just be mindful that you are now engaged in a fight and if caught, you will *both* be punished. If fighting back just isn't an option, then go to your folks, or your closest family member, or a teacher and tell them everything. This isn't 'ratting.' You shouldn't have to put up with crap like this, so go to an adult you trust. They will know what to do, and you must allow them to help. I hope that answers your question okay young man, and please feel free to chat to me later if you need to.'

I feel like utter crap. I use the cover of the round of applause to make my way out of the school without anyone noticing. I trudge home, the words from that speaker buzzing around my head. I need Justin to know I'm sorry. Yeah! That's what I need to do. I turn on my heels and confidently stride back towards the school in the hope of seeing Justin. I know he comes home this way. How do I know? Because I've chased him so many times.

It's not long before I spot Justin waiting to cross the road. I freeze, and as he looks up, our eyes meet. In that very moment, I wanted to completely burst out crying, drop to my knees, and beg for forgiveness. But I'll never do that. So, I just turned and walked away.

Wednesday: 7.43 pm

I'm up in the room I share with my younger brother. He's outside causing mayhem, so I am thankful for the moment of peace. My da started as soon as I walked in earlier, but this time? This time he was met with the same smarmy attitude and aggression I usually keep for Justin.

'Say whatever ya want, ya sap. If you think the words of an alco who can't even hold down a job in a bread factory are going to get to me anymore? You're wrong ... daddy! I don't give a rats-arse what you think of me, because it couldn't be any worse than how I currently think of myself. But I'm gonna make this right. And I'm gonna stop being like me da ... an arsehole.'

He came lunging at me after that last statement. My ma grabbed hold of him, and roared at me to get up to my room.

'With pleasure,' I reply. And this is where I've been since, staring at the white, A4 page in front of me. I have decided to write Justin a letter. I haven't gotten very far yet, but I am determined to get this done.

And as I sit here on my own, the only words I have written so far play over and over in my mind:

Howya Justin, It's David (D-Man) here. Justin, I am so, so sorry ...

Discuss

♦ Should Justin have told his dad sooner?

♦ Was Justin right to try to stick up for himself in the toilet?

♦ Does David have an excuse as to why he is so horrible to Justin, because of his home life?

♦ Did you notice how Justin's dad praises him, whereas David's dad runs him down? Is this Justin's fault?

These are just some of the questions I came up with as I wrote this chapter for you. I'm sure you have many more, so please don't be afraid to ask them. Feel free to write down your thoughts on this chapter in the Personal Reflections section at the back of this book.

Sadly, this chapter is based on two students I met during my talks. Neither of them knows the other, but they both showed such bravery as they spoke to me about what was going on in their lives. The student who was being bullied, 'Justin' in this story, filled my heart with sadness. He is such an intelligent, funny young man, but some bully decided he was his next target. It destroyed him. But his dad stepped in and, instead of going around battering people, his dad focused all of his attention on his son. He made sure, daily, that his son believed in himself, loved himself, and became happy with the person he is.

If you are strong in your mind, if you fully believe in yourself and you are happy and grateful for all you've got, then no negative opinions that are aimed towards you will penetrate your armour. But fists and kicks will, right? I get that. I just can't sit here and tell you to go around hitting people. All I know is, nobody should be hitting anybody. Instead, I recommend getting as many adults involved as possible. Start with your family, your closest friend, or a teacher, and allow them to do whatever they feel they need to do to help you. This is not your fault. And asking for help is not a sign of weakness – it is a sign of strength.

Now, what about David (D-man)? He's not a very nice guy right? And there are no excuses for his behaviour.

David was inspired by the other student I met who blew me away with his honesty. He told me, to my face, that he is (was) a bully! I was shocked, but kinda impressed with his honesty. He was crying when he told me, so I knew he wasn't entirely happy with being a bully. I knew there was hope. I spent some time chatting with this lad, and his honesty about his home life shocked and saddened me at the same time. His dad is a drinker who doesn't seem to like his own son very much. I knew I could help this young lad with his self-esteem, but I could sense he was using his shitty family situation as an excuse to be a bully. I shot that down!

There is never, ever an excuse to bully anyone. I gave you a snapshot of the bully's life in the above story to show that even if your own situation is really bad, you can't just take it out on others. Bullying should never, ever, be tolerated. If you have a shitty home life, then I am truly sorry for you. But that doesn't give you the right to hurt others. Instead, you must seek as much help as possible. And again, this doesn't make you weak, it makes you strong. So go and talk to someone and tell them everything. It's never too late to become a better person.

If you find yourself being bullied, please reach out and ask for help. What you are going through is hard, but know this: It's not your fault. There are numbers and websites at the back of this book, so please use them.

If you know of someone being bullied, offer your support – let them know you are there and you care. I know it may seem like it's 'none of your business', but what if it was you being bullied? Wouldn't you want as much help as possible?

And if you are actually bullying someone? Stop right now. It is wrong on so many levels. Stop, apologise, and move forward in your life with positivity. You are better than that.

9.

'No One Understands ...' – Gráinne's Story

I'm not sure when these feelings started. I cannot pinpoint the day, hour and second when my mind became consumed by these thoughts. Thoughts of loneliness and unending sadness. Thoughts of fear and loathing. Thoughts of never fitting in and feeling like a freak. Thoughts that are slowly chipping away at my soul. I look around me every day and all I feel is envy and guilt. God. I'm such a bad person, aren't I? I mean, I should be happy for my friends and all they have going on in their lives. But instead, I feel envy and sadness. I'm such a bitch.

Even my closest friend, Paula, has no idea of how messed up my brain feels. We have been friends almost ten years now. We met when we were both just seven years of age. I had literally only moved into a new housing estate with my family when, within minutes, I found myself in the front garden of my new home playing with the girl who was to become my best friend. Paula is the total opposite to me in so many ways, yet we just seem to click. She has brown hair, I have blonde hair. She is loud and fun, whereas I am shy and, I dunno, boring I suppose. For almost ten years now, we have built a friendship to be proud of.

'You are my rock, Gráinne,' are the words I hear most days from Paula, and yet, I cannot tell her how I feel right now. I can't tell anyone, not even my family. I've got a pretty normal family I guess. I don't come from a broken home and thankfully I have never experienced abuse in any shape or form. I love my family deeply – they just don't 'get' me. And it hurts when I allow myself to think that that they *just couldn't be arsed trying to 'get' me.'* They don't understand.

No one understands.

It's Saturday morning. I wake up, and for a brief moment I feel completely normal. A bit sleepy yes, but normal nonetheless. But it doesn't take long for the ill feelings to slowly find their way back into my mind. *I hate myself – I hate my life...* These words bounce around my brain like a pinball being fired into a pinball machine. What is wrong with me?

I force myself out of my bed and throw on my dressing gown. I make my way down the stairs and can hear my younger brother and my mam singing along to a song being played on the radio in our kitchen. *'Uptown funk gonna' give it to ya. Saturday night and we in the spot. Don't believe me just watch...'* I watch at the kitchen door as my mam and my brother Gerry sing this line from the Bruno Mars song, and then break into a silly dance together. I smile.

'Ah heya sleepy-head,' chirps my mam when she spots me at the door. 'Breakfast?'

'No, I'll make my own in a bit. Thanks mam,' I say.

'Wanna dance with me?', asks Gerry.

'God no! Ugh. You're so annoying sometimes Gerry,' comes my harsh reply. Harsh is actually an understatement. Gerry is actually a cool little brother. Yes he irritates me to distraction sometimes, but isn't that what younger brothers are meant to do?

'You're always in a bad mood lately,' comes Gerry's grumpy reply.

'Yeah? Well, what's it to you huh? Why does it bother *you* so much Gerry eh? Feck off you little creep and mind your own business.' I almost shout this at poor Gerry. His face drops.

My mam intervenes. '*Gráinne!* Don't speak to your brother like that. He's only trying to have a bit of fun with you for Christ sake!' Mam sounds really pissed off with me.

I feel guilty, but instead of saying sorry, I just scream, 'Leave me alone the lot of you. Not one of you has a clue!'

'Gráinne...' I hear my mam call my name, but I choose to ignore her. Instead, I make my way to my room, slam the door closed behind me, and fall face first onto one of my soft pillows. I am sobbing uncontrollably. What is going on with me?

'Gráinne?' My mam is outside my door.

'Go away mam,' I shout back through my tears.

'Gráinne ... look. I'm sorry if we upset you. Come on. Please come back downstairs and have some breakfast with us.'

'Please mam. Just leave me alone for now will you? I'm okay.' I ask this of my mam whilst lying to her at the same time. I am far from okay. I am sick of everything. I am sick of this life.

Saturday afternoon and myself and Paula are sitting in Costa Coffee having a frappuccino and sharing a blueberry muffin. 'So then, I was like, *'eh ... do I have "mug" wrote across my face? Get the boat you fool.'* I feel a little guilty. I know Paula is talking about her 'on again/off again/on ... *again*' boyfriend Stuart, but I shamefully have zero interest. It's not long before Paula cops this. 'Eh, am I boring you Gráinne?' she asks.

'Sorry Paula, no. Not at all,' I offer as a reply.

'You sure you're okay?' I can actually hear the concern in my best friend's voice. Isn't that all I'm looking for? Someone who cares? And yet, I *still* lie straight to her face.

'Yeah – sorry. I just had a little run-in with mam this morning. No biggie. Sorry. Go on, tell me what he did after you said that to him.'

'Are you sure you're okay Gráinne,' asks Paula, 'are you sure that's all that is wrong? Like, I hope you know you can tell me anything.'

'I know Paula, I know. But I'm grand,' I lie. God, lying is becoming so easy for me lately. 'Please, just continue telling me about what happened with you and Stuart.'

'Well, once you're sure? Okay. So then, I was like ...'

Almost instantly I once again zone out. Now, my thoughts are further consumed by my guilt. I've just told my best friend one of the biggest lies I have ever told her – *'I'm fine.'*

Why can't I tell her? What is wrong with me? I hate myself.

Saturday evening and my Aunty Annie has dropped in to see my mam. My mam and Annie are sisters. Aunty Annie is pretty cool I guess. She is a bit mad sometimes, but her heart is huge and she would do anything for you. We've always had a good relationship. I always felt I could tell her anything. Maybe I could talk to her about these thoughts that are bombarding me. And yet, all it takes is a simple statement of concern from Aunty Antoinette and I immediately shut down.

'So, Gráinne, your mam was saying you both had a little tiff earlier. I think she's worried missus. Are you okay? Is there anything going on that you wanna talk to me about? There is nothing you can't tell me Gráinne. I'll never judge you, nor will I give out to you.'

I can feel myself about to burst into tears. These are the words I've been waiting to hear right? Aunty Annie is offering me exactly what I want. Yet, the dark voice that has taken up residency in my mind becomes over-bearing. *'She won't get it. She'll think you're a fuck-up. She will never understand.'* So, I do what, shamefully, I have become a pro at lately – I lie.

'Yeah Aunty Annie, I'm fine. I was just being a hormonal teenager this morning. Like you've never been like that before.' I fake a laugh as I make this last assessment, which seems to do the trick.

'Oh, I was a right moody cow when I was younger alright, 'starts Aunty Annie, 'just once you're okay? And once you know you can talk to me … anytime.'

'I know I can, thanks Aunty Annie.' Again, I lie. I'm such a shitty person.

Saturday night and my mind is made up. I can't be here anymore. I can't take feeling worthless anymore. Feeling like I am trying to compete with other girls, and failing miserably each and every time. All I do lately is cause worry and upset. My mam and dad, my brother, my entire family would be better off if I was just 'not here' anymore. Not to mention my friends. I mean, they all have great lives. Boyfriends, great hair, great clothes. All I offer them is depression and sadness. Especially Paula. All I've ever wanted is for Paula to be happy. But she will never be happy with me around. All I do is drag people down. I can't do this anymore. I want it all to end.

I pick up my blue biro and begin writing my letter to my folks. I decide to spend the night writing these final words of mine, and then tomorrow evening? I will do everyone a favour and ... I am crying harder than I have ever cried. One lonely tear hits the A4 page and smudges my opening line:

'Mam, Dad. I am so sorry ...'

The screech of pain in my Aunty Annie's voice wakes me from my slumber. I rub the sleep out of my eyes, and try to focus. 'Ah Rita (my mam's name), what the hell has he done? Why Rita? *Why?*' I have never heard my Aunty Annie so upset. She is actually banging something downstairs. I even hear Gerry getting upset. I jump from my bed, and as I do, my pillow falls to the floor, exposing the letter I eventually constructed last night. I shudder for a second, then remind myself that what I am going to do this evening is for the best. I hide the letter in my desk drawer and make my way out of my room.

I walk into the kitchen and see my Aunty Annie hunched over, crying like I've never seen her cry before. 'Aunty Annie?' I say.

'Gráinne ... ah Gráinne.' Aunty Annie is finding it hard to talk.

My dad has taken her softly into his arms, and he has now led her into our sitting room for a chat. He closes the door behind him, and as he does, I turn to my mam and say, 'What the hell is going on mam. Why is Aunty Annie so upset?' I can see my mam is also crying. What the hell is going on?

'You know Aunty Annie's best friend, Zoe?', starts my mam, 'Well, em ...' My mam is completely and utterly distraught as she tries to gather the words to tell me. 'Em ... Zoe's son? He's a year older than you, Gráinne. Oh Gráinne ... they found him this morning. He took his own life.' My mam collapses onto one of the small oak chairs that match our kitchen table. Jesus. Oh god! Look at her. Look at how upset she is. Oh god! I run over to my mam and throw my arms around her, and as I do, I hear my Aunty Annie let out the saddest, most chilling cry I have ever heard her make: *'Why?!? Why did he do this?*

Jesus. Look at how upset my mam, dad and Aunty Annie are. And this poor boy is not even a member of our family! Just look at the devastation this news has caused. I kinda knew the lad. He was good looking, he seemed pretty chilled, and just sort of kept to himself ... just like me. Oh god. How incredibly sad. He's actually gone now – forever. I think of the note that is hidden in the drawer of my desk. I look at my mam and how the news of a boy she hardly knew taking his own life has quite literally shattered her. Imagine how she would feel if that boy was me? Oh god.

Tuesday morning and it is the day of this tragic young man's funeral. I told my Aunty Annie that I would be right by her side for the whole day. She hasn't really talked much in the last few days. She is super close to her friend Zoe. Just like myself and Paula, they too are friends from childhood. Aunty Annie was there the day this young man came into the world, and now she needs to be strong for her friend as she tries to come to terms with his loss.

I have never seen our church so full. This lad was a promising GAA player and it seems the whole club has turned up. There is a horrible, eerie sadness hanging over the entire church. Nobody is talking. All that can be heard is sobbing, and angry statements. I see some of the really cool lads from our village all sitting in a line on one of the church's pews. They are completely distraught. They've just lost a best friend. I see Zoe at the top of the church. She is broken. In fact, when the priest signals the start of the mass by instructing us to bless ourselves, I hear a gasp coming from the top of the church. Zoe has collapsed. The entire church is now sobbing. The weight and gravity of this situation has suddenly smacked me in the face. I look at Zoe, and all I can see is my own mam. I look around the church and all I can see are people falling to pieces. I think again of that letter I wrote some days back – oh god!

The mass was one of the saddest experiences of my young life. As the coffin was carried out of the church, it left behind a wake of devastation. I am standing in the grounds waiting on my chance to embrace Zoe. As I stand waiting in line, I hear one of the lads say, 'Maybe we'll hold a match for him in his honour, or name a trophy after him down in the club.' I could see this young lad was saying this, through his tears, from a good place. But sadly, Zoe's dad (the tragic young man's grandfather) has taken exception.

'And just what in the hell will that do eh? A match? A fucking trophy? Is all of that crap going to bring my grandson back? No! Of course it won't. A trophy you say? Don't be so stupid. Nothing will bring him back ...'

I can see the shock on this young lad's face as Zoe's father rips into him. But as soon as Zoe's father stops talking, he erupts into tears, and this young lad throws his arms around him.

'I'm sorry son,' Zoe's father says, 'I didn't mean to shout at you. I know you mean well. We're just hurting so much son. He wrote in his letter than *'no one understands'* ... for Christ sake! Why couldn't he try us you know? I always thought he knew he could come to me. But now? Now he will never know the damage he has done, or the number of people he has hurt. But more importantly, now he will never know how much he touched us all with his spirit. Now he'll never know how much we love him, or how much we're going to miss him. He wrote that *no one understands*? Well, he's right. Because I can't understand what the hell is going on right now.'

These words from Zoe's father have drilled their way into my head. I feel a tidal wave of guilt wash over me. I look over at my Aunty Annie and see her holding Zoe in her arms. I crumble.

I walk away to be alone for a moment. I am consumed once again by guilt and ill feelings. But this time my guilt and ill feelings are about what I was actually contemplating. I'm not sure what happened next, but I suddenly find myself with my phone in my hand. I launch my internet browser and as soon as I see the familiar logo of Google, I proceed to type my search into the search bar – 'teen suicide helpline'. The top hit is the number 1800 247 247 for Pieta House. I hit call. I'm shaking.

'Hello? How can I help you?' The friendly sounding voice instantly puts me at ease.

'I am so messed up,' I say, 'I was about to take my own life ...'

A lot of time has passed since that sad Tuesday morning. 'Time is a great healer,' they say, but I wouldn't dare say that to Zoe. She has never recovered. I heard Aunty Annie telling my mam how worried she is about Zoe. She informed my mam that Zoe has begun drinking during the day, and most days can be found drunk by 6.oo pm. It's just so sad. And to think – I was going to inflict this on my own family too.

The best thing I have ever done is make that phone call to Pieta House. I was instantly made to feel like the only human being on the planet, and soon an entire plan of action was put into place for me. I still attend counselling sessions (both group and one-on-one), and I am so grateful for them. Slowly, that dark voice that occupied my mind is leaving for good. 'Rome wasn't built in a day' and all that, but I am making progress. The team in Pieta House even gave me the strength to tell my family. I'm sure you can imagine their shock. In the beginning, this shock was almost portrayed as anger. *Why didn't you come to us? Why?* But as a family, we are working through it and every day we are becoming even closer.

I ripped that letter I wrote into a million pieces. I had convinced myself that *'no one understands'* when the truth is, I never allowed them the opportunity to even *try* to understand. Today, I talk to *everyone* about how I am feeling – good or bad. It is so important to talk. It is so important to share your worries and fears.

I know if Zoe could talk right now, she would completely agree with me. Poor Zoe. She will never be the same again. She will *never* understand.

Discuss

◆ Was Grainne right to keep these horrible feelings to herself?

◆ Did she have family and friends that she could turn to?

◆ Was Zoe's father right for giving out to the young lad outside the church?

These are just some of the questions I came up with as I wrote this chapter for you. I'm sure you have many more, so please don't be afraid to ask them. Feel free to write down your thoughts on this chapter in the Personal Reflections section at the back of this book.

I struggled writing this chapter. The fact that we are losing so many young men and women to suicide these days is something that weighs heavily on my mind, as I'm sure it does with you. In the Introduction to this book, I told you all about a girl named 'K,' and how the story of her friend taking his own life, at thirteen, had a massive impact on me. It inspired me to write this book. And I always knew I was going to try to tackle this issue ... but I really struggled. During my time in prison, two people I knew took their own lives, and to this day I find myself left with a massive lump in my throat at just the mention of their names. We have an alarmingly high number of suicides in this country, and lately young people have become a significant part of this statistic.

I feel I must address something at this point. I was stunned recently when a lady I know told me what she overheard at the funeral of a young man who had tragically taken his own life. Two young lads were in front of her, and one turned to the other and said, 'I wonder would I get a turnout like this at my funeral...' That is just shocking. To think that a young person would even entertain thoughts like that is completely wrong. Life is for living, not wondering how many would attend your funeral. If you ever have dark thoughts like this, please seek help immediately. This shocks and scares me at the same time. We need to start a conversation about this. We need to come together and try to do all we can to eradicate this once and for all.

If you can relate in any way to Gráinne in this story, I urge you to seek help now! Put this book down and go and find the adult you trust the most. It doesn't matter who it is. Go right now and tell them everything. Don't allow the voice in your mind to control you. No difficulties in this life are permanent – none! If you are struggling with issues, sometimes it feels like they are never going to go away, or you will never feel better. But this simply is not true. The sun rises every morning without fail. And this sun offers a brand new day for you to live, a brand new day for you to express how you feel and share your emotions. The importance of talking about your thoughts, no matter how dark or crazy you might think they are, has never been more prevalent than it is today. It really is 'okay not to be okay'.

If you feel that you have no one to turn to, then reach out for help. In this story I mentioned Pieta House – these guys are just incredible – but if they are not for you, then go to the back of this book and you will see a variety of numbers and websites to contact. Please use them.

If you have lost someone through suicide, the same importance of talking and sharing your feelings applies. You will feel so many mixed emotions – anger, sadness, loss, love – that sometimes it's easy to feel a bit lost yourself. So I beg you ... start a conversation about it. Talk to your family, your friends, your teachers. Share your fears and anger and sadness and allow them to do the same if they need to.

Please don't ever suffer in silence.

10.

'You Are Enough!'

When I decided to write this book, I had one mission. I wanted the reader to truly believe the words: I Am Enough! And as you read this final chapter, I really hope that is how you are feeling.

We've dealt with some thorny issues, haven't we? From peer pressure to consent. From drug use to losing someone. And the topics I chose are just *some* of the issues that have come up countless times in the numerous schools and Youthreach groups I have been so lucky to address.

I said at the very beginning of this book that I refuse to believe that the youth of today are just being 'moody and rude' for absolutely no reason. I believe that this generation experiences immense pressure, and many find it so difficult to express their true feelings. So when I am speaking with the adults in my life, I always stick up for you guys. I fight your corner and try as best as I can to give these adults some food for thought.

I always say, *'If your son/daughter/nephew/niece is being moody and rude, I urge you to sit them down and ask,*

"Why?" But when you do? Clear your mind and your heart and listen with intent.'

This is what I decided to do when I first began speaking in schools and Youthreach groups, and as a result this book was born. I found that if I took the time to listen intently to the young adults in front of me, while offering no judgement, they in turn would open up even more. But it has been upsetting to realise how much some of you are suffering.

I'm on your side, but I need you to do something for me. I need you to think about how *you* are and how *you* act when it comes to the adults in your life. The relationship you have with adults is a two-way street. If you want them to listen to you, you have got to look at how you are with them too. I bet there has been a time when you actually *were* 'moody and rude' for no reason. I know I was, countless times, when I was in my teens. You are going through hormonal changes in your body and these changes can have you feeling all sorts of things. So try to be mindful of your own mood, and go easy on your teachers too! I know it may seem like they have literally 'got it in for you', but I promise that is just not true. They are only doing their job. So a little give and take between yourself and your teachers or Youthreach leaders will go a long way.

All the advice I have given throughout these pages I have actually had to use on myself too. There have been moments in my life when I have completely hated myself. There have been times that I wished I 'wasn't here'. I never felt good enough. But I also need to 'own my shit'. Instead of seeking the help I clearly needed, I shut myself off and convinced myself that I was fine – that everyone else had a problem, not me. I blamed all my problems on others, and as a result, I became a really shitty person. I failed as a son, a friend, and a father. I became an alcoholic. I foolishly believed that all my sorrows would evaporate once I was drunk. But all I was doing was pushing the guilt, ill feeling and depression further down into the pit of my stomach, until one day there was no room for more. Today, I offer no excuses for how much of an arsehole I was, but I am hoping my actions in the future will speak volumes. It is never too late to change.

The one thing that *is* kind of embarrassing for me is that I needed to go to prison to 'find myself'. But find myself I did, and I am now so very proud of the man I have become. But it took a hell of a lot of work! I realised the need to talk about my feelings. I needed to be okay with asking for help. I needed to believe, every single day, that *I Am Enough*!

I want to leave you with an idea. What I am about to share with you is something I do myself, every single night. One of my favourite words in the English language is *gratitude*. The expression of gratitude is one of the best things you will ever do. Why? Because when you express gratitude, you are filled with happy thoughts and feelings. It's as simple as that. So give this a go.

Get yourself a pen and a journal of some sort. Now some of you might be saying, 'Eh, I'll use my phone, thank you very much.' But I urge you not to. You use that bloody thing for everything else, so for this exercise please use a pen and some paper. The feeling of connection between your hand, the pen and the paper is a unique experience.

Once you have your journal or diary, you might name it your 'Gratitude Journal'. Now, once you are tucked up in bed, simply write down the things you are grateful for on that particular day. There is no set number of things you can write, in fact, the more the merrier. Allow yourself to experience the happy feelings as they flow through you, all from writing something like, *'I am so grateful for my family.'* or *'I have such great friends'*. Spend at least five minutes doing this and I promise you will drift off into dream land in a much happier place. And when you wake up? Have a quick glance at what made you feel grateful yesterday, and see what new things will be added to your journal today. I do this every day and it works wonders. You see? Even us adults need some help believing that we are enough.

To get started, you might write down your thoughts in the Personal Reflections section at the back of this book.

So, we're near the end. And my final piece of advice you've heard before: Let's get talking to each other guys. Let's open a dialog with our family, our friends, our teachers. Let's share how we feel in a confident manner. Don't be afraid to spark a conversation about a topic from this book with an adult. Ask them for their perspective. Remember, they were once teens too. Some may even be able to relate to the issues highlighted in this book, and they may offer you some sound advice.

But talk guys – talk to each other. Talk to me. Talk to everyone. Don't ever suffer in silence.

Finally, at the very end of this book after the Personal Reflections section I have included a simple 'Certificate of Completion'. As you can see, I wrote a little poem for you, and there is a space for you to put your name. I would love for you to cut out this cert and place it somewhere where you will see it every morning when you get up. And as you get yourself ready for the day, please read out these few words, and believe in every single one of them. Because:

You – Absolutely – Are Enough!

Acknowledgements

♦ To my mam – my 'Ninja'. I am the man I am today because of how you reared me, and how you have loved and continue to love me. I love being with you, and I love listening to your stories. But most of all, I love YOU mam. You are amazing Lily, and I am beyond grateful for you. Thank you for always being there for me – even when I made it so hard for you. You are amazing mam.

♦ To Antoinette – my 'Reason'. What can I say that hasn't already been said? You have believed in me from day one, and encouraged me in every aspect of my life. I am the best version of me because of you. I never thought I deserved to find true love, but in you, I have found the truest, most pure love known to man. You are my everything, and I love you with all I've got. Thank you for being my best friend. You blow me away.

♦ To my brothers – you are three of the strongest men I know. Even though my past didn't allow our relationships to form, none of you have ever held that against me. And today, I class the three of you as, not only my brothers, but my amazing friends too. Gerry, Noel and Jason ... I love you all deeply. Thank you.

♦ To my sisters-in-law – you are all incredible, strong, amazing women. My brothers may have got lucky the day they met you, but my entire family got lucky the day you came into our lives. Barbara, Bernadette and Niamh, you all rock! And you gave me my amazing nephews and nieces

Acknowledgements

whom I adore too (Paul, Mark, Alan, Jenny, Sean, Conor, Sarah, Luke, Adam and Dylan ... you are all amazing).

♦ To 'Mammy Love' and all of Antoinette's family – you lot are incredible, and I honestly cannot believe how luck I am to have inherited such an amazing 'second family.' Angela, Susan, David (yep, even you Dave), Josh, Cody, Craig and Taylor, I love you all so much and I am truly grateful for you – yep, even you Dave! But my biggest amount of gratitude goes to the head of the family, 'Mammy Love'. You are one of the most calming, understanding, and patient humans I have ever met, and the love you offer is second to none. I love you so much Anne. Thank you for making me feel so welcome, and supporting myself and your daughter as we traverse this life. You are amazing.

♦ To Mick, Ash, Cian and Callum – you guys are just – wow! I know it must be strange for you all to see a book from me that is not about you! I always say 'everything happens for a reason,' and how I met you, Mick, is a perfect example of that. But today, not only have I inherited the greatest friend a bloke could ask for, I have also inherited the love and friendship of his wife, and I have become 'Uncle Gary' to two of the most amazing boys this world has ever seen. Ash, Cian and Callum, I adore you all. Thank you for always being there for me. And as for you 'Fitzer?' You are one of the best things that has ever happened to me, and you have no idea how much you truly saved my life. I absolutely love you unconditionally – and I love the fact you are now mortified reading this!

♦ To David and Darina – Wow! Who would have thought that my story about the most shameful time of my life would lead me to The Liffey Press and straight into the embrace of both yourself and Darina. You gave me a shot when no one else was willing to risk it Dave (or Boss as I like to call you). You took a massive risk with me, and I will forever be in your debt. But to think that today, I can proudly call both yourself and Darina my friends, is something that still catches my breath. I adore you both so much. I adore your two amazing sons, and I am beyond grateful for everything you have given me. And *when* the film of *Joys of Joy* comes out? I can't wait to look at you both, and simply smile. Thank you guys. I love ya's!!!!!!! (the ! are for you Boss).

♦ To Frank and Rachel – both of you are actually extended gifts from David and Darina. Let me start with you Rachel. Wow – what an amazing lady you truly are. And it's clear ol' Franky-Boy is punching above his weight too! Although we haven't spent as much time together as I have with your hubby, every moment I do spend with you is truly special. Thank you for always making me feel so good about myself. You rock! And as for you Frank? I am your biggest fan. You have absolutely no idea how much you have inspired me. Your skills are there for the world to see, and to watch you soar lately has been an honour. But what you bring into my life as a friend cannot be meassured. You are a modern-day hero in my eyes, and I am beyond proud to call you my friend. And as for our future? Well, it looks bright sir. As we always say: Onwards!

♦ To James and Juanita – I still find the need to pinch myself when I think of why you two beautiful humans are in my life. I will never be able to fully express my gratitude to you both – but I'm going to try bloody hard to do so! From the bottom of my heart, thank you.

♦ To Deborah – I adore you ... my very own fairytale. You have no idea how much you play a massive part in my story, and I will never be able to articulate what you truly mean to me. I love you, Gerry, and the kids with all I've got. Thank you so much M'lady.

♦ To Dee – Ahh Dee. The one person were I say, 'ahh, wait until you meet Dee … she will blow you away.' And when they do meet you? That is exactly what you do. I love, love, LOVE you so much, and I am so thankful for you and all you bring.

♦ To Eilish – 'me buddy!' I adore you – allow that to sink in for a second….Your friendship is everything to me. You have inspired me, moved me, but most importantly, made me laugh – A *lot* – when I needed it most. What a woman, what a friend. I feckin' *love ya*!

♦ To Maggie – Jaysis Mags! You didn't think I'd forget you now did ya? When I think of our story – how we met – I can't help but smile. You are one of the most talented, creative beings this planet has ever seen, and I cannot wait for us to begin working together. I know we are going to create something special. Thank you for being my friend, for loving me, and for allowing me to love you back.

♦ To Grace and 'The Ballymahon Crew' – Grace, you are one of the strongest, most inspiring ladies I have had the pleasure of meeting. You're a Ninja. 'The Ballymahon Crew' – You lot are simply incredible. A bunch of teens who have inspired and moved me beyond comprehension. And every single one of you are, *more than enough*. Thank you all for blowing my mind.

♦ To Jenny and Samantha – Jenny, thank you for your constant stream of support since day one, and for slagging the life out of me at the drop of a hat! Samantha, thank you for your advice, comments and encouragement. ('keeping up with the Jones? I'm such an aul fella aren't I lol). And both of you please give my love to Conor, and an extra big hug to my hero, Oscar.

♦ To all the amazing folks who have followed and supported me on social media – I am so proud to call you all my friends, and I am so proud of the positivity we have created with my 'Monday Posts'. You're all amazing and I am so grateful for each and every one of you.

♦ To Karina and Aunua Academy – Where do I start? Karina, you are my 'sister from another mister,' a real life Mary Poppins. The reason you started Aunua alone shows the world what an incredible woman you are. You have brought nothing but happiness into my world since we met, and you also brought Danielle with you too – another Ninja whom I am so grateful for. But making me an Ambassador of Aunua Academy is still an honour I am trying to come to terms with. Wow. I hope you enjoyed the little 'Aunua plug' in the book too. I love you (and you Danielle) so, so much. Thank you.

♦ To Sharon, Hannah and Luke – Luke? You're a legend young man. Keep doing and believing in you, because you *rock*! Hannah? Your skills as an artist are there for all to see. Added to that is that fact you are a complete Ninja! You amaze and inspire me missus ... never change. Sharon? Words cannot describe the admiration I have for you. You are an amazing friend (to Lily too – she loves ya), and an incredible mother. You're doing a wonderful job and should feel super proud of yourself. I know I'm proud to call you my friend.

♦ To Dave Saunders, founder of 'Lads To Dads' – Dave, my admiration for you has gone through the roof. What you are currently trying to do for young men in this country is simply incredible. And on a personal level, what you have done for me is just ... wow! Keep on keeping on sir – this is only the beginning.

Acknowledgements

◆ To the teachers and staff in every school and Youthreach group I have had the honour to speak in – the way you made me feel so welcome is something that still brings a tear to my eye. From the teachers I spoke to that day in Listowel, to Paul and his colleges in the Youhtreach in Dundalk, you have all blown me away. A special mention to Nicola, Caroline, Charlene, Allison and Caoimhe (the stalker!) to name but a very small few. My admiration for you all goes through the roof, and I feel a lot more confident knowing our youths are in your capable hands. Thank you all from the bottom of my heart, and I really I hope to see you all again soon.

◆ To the students, teens, and young adults I have had the honour to meet – *wow*! Do you know what is crazy? Not one of you truly knows the impact you have had on me. The respect each and every one of you have shown me is something that I had convinced myself I didn't deserve. Each and every one of you has made *me feel that I am enough*. I will always have your back, and I know together we can make a difference. Thank you, each and every one of you, from the bottom of my heart. You are all Ninjas!

◆ Lastly, I want to thank *you*, the person reading this. I obviously want to thank you for your support, that goes without saying. But moreover, I want to thank you for coming on this journey with me, and for allowing yourself to feel certain things that may have been alien to you. I want to thank you for your strength and your spirit. But most of all, I want to thank you for being *you*.

Telephone Numbers and Websites You May Find Useful

- **Samaritans Hotline:** 116 123 or text, 087 260 9090

- **Pieta House:** www.pieta.ie This website has a ton of information and avenues of help for you. Head to the 'Contact' section for a list of numbers and services near you.

- **Cycle Against Suicide:** www.cycleagainstsuicide.com The work this organisation does is simply incredible. This site will offer you many avenues and options on a range of mental health issues.

- **Aunua Academy:** www.aunuaacademy.com Yes, I am plugging my own here, but everything available to you on Aunua's site is completely free.

- **Ditch The Label:** www.ditchthelabel.org This site offers a wide variety of help and knowledge when it comes to all aspects of bullying.

- **Jigsaw** – Young People's Health In Mind: www.jigsaw.ie This site is one I found a lot of the groups I have spoken to found to be quite useful.

- **Spunout:** www.spunout.ie This site is like a 'one-stop shop' for all the numbers, websites etc that relate to you and your mental health.

These are not necessarily 'the best' sites and numbers, just the ones I have some level of experience with. What I found amazing as I researched these sites is that with just a quick Google search you can find the help you need almost immediately.

Personal Reflections

Reflections on Ch. 1: 'Am I Enough?' – Martin's Story

_____

_____

_____

_____

_____

_____

_____

_____

Reflections on Ch. 2: 'Sure, All Your Friends Are Doing It ...' – Megan's Story

_____

_____

_____

_____

_____

_____

_____

Reflections on Ch. 3 – 'The Importance of Family and Friends' – Doug and Josh's Story

_____

_____

_____

_____

_____

_____

_____

Reflections on Ch. 4: (Un)Social Media

(1) Cyberbullying/Trolling

_____

_____

_____

_____

_____

(2) Negative Body Image

_____

_____

_____

_____

_____

_____

(3) The Human Connection

_____

_____

_____

_____

_____

_____

_____

(4) Privacy and 'Likes'

_____

_____

_____

_____

_____

_____

_____

(5) Online Safety

_____

_____

_____

_____

_____

_____

Reflections on Ch. 5 – 'It's Just Not Worth It' *– Jimmy's Story*

_____

_____

_____

_____

_____

_____

_____

_____

Reflections on Ch. 6: 'I Will Always Miss You ...' *– Josh's Story*

_____

_____

_____

_____

_____

_____

_____

_____

_____

_____

_____

_____

Reflections on Ch. 7 – 'No Means No' – Maeve's Story

_____

_____

_____

_____

_____

_____

_____

_____

Reflections on Ch. 8: 'The Bully and the Bullied' – Justin and David's Story

_____

_____

_____

_____

_____

_____

_____

_____

_____

_____

Reflections on Ch. 9 – 'No One Understands ...' – *Gráinne's Story*

_____

_____

_____

_____

_____

_____

_____

_____

Things I Am Grateful For

_____

_____

_____

_____

_____

_____

_____

_____

_____

_____

_____

CERTIFICATE

OF

COMPLETION

I AM ONE OF A KIND
I'M SO PROUD TO BE ME
AND TODAY I WANT
THE WHOLE WORLD TO SEE
THAT EVEN WHEN
THIS LIFE GETS TOUGH,

I,_____

KNOW THAT,

I AM ENOUGH

Congratulations
YOU ROCK!